Multiracial Cosmotheandrism

Multiracial Cosmotheandrism

A Practical Theology of Multiracial Experiences

Aizaiah G. Yong

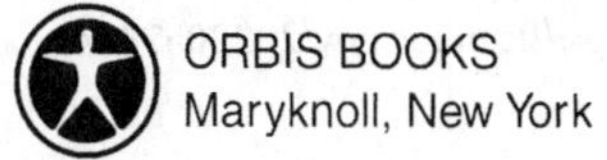
ORBIS BOOKS
Maryknoll, New York

Founded in 1970, Orbis Books endeavors to publish works that enlighten the mind, nourish the spirit, and challenge the conscience. The publishing arm of the Maryknoll Fathers and Brothers, Orbis seeks to explore the global dimensions of the Christian faith and mission, to invite dialogue with diverse cultures and religious traditions, and to serve the cause of reconciliation and peace. The books published reflect the views of their authors and do not represent the official position of the Maryknoll Society. To learn more about Orbis Books, please visit our website at www.orbisbooks.com.

Published by Orbis Books, P.O. Box 302, Maryknoll, NY 10545-0302.

Manufactured in the United States of America

Library of Congress Cataloging-in-Publication Data

Names: Yong, Aizaiah G., author.
Title: Multiracial cosmotheandrism : a practical theology of multiracial experiences / Aizaiah G. Yong.
Description: Maryknoll, NY : Orbis Books, [2023] | Includes bibliographical references and index. | Summary: "A practical theology of mysticism that centers multiracial experience and spiritual practice"—Provided by publisher.
Identifiers: LCCN 2022057383 (print) | LCCN 2022057384 (ebook) | ISBN 9781626985254 (trade paperback) | ISBN 9781608339860 (epub)
Subjects: LCSH: Race relations—Religious aspects—Christianity. | Racially mixed people—Religious life—United States. | Minorities—Religious life—United States. | Trinity. | Mysticism. | United States—Race relations—Religious aspects. | Panikkar, Raimon, 1918-2010
Classification: LCC BL65.R3 .Y66 2023 (print) | LCC BL65.R3 (ebook) | DDC 230.089—dc23/eng/20230310
LC record available at https://lccn.loc.gov/2022057383
LC ebook record available at https://lccn.loc.gov/2022057384

I dedicate this work to my lifelong partner,
Nereyda (Neddy), and my children, Serenity Joy,
Valor Amoz, Río Joseph, and Kairo Ricardo,
who are all mixed along with me.
You are my greatest inspiration!
Thank you for the laughter, joy, surprise,
and endless love you bring to my life.
To my children, as you continue to live out
and bear witness to the beauty, mystery, and
diversity of the multiracial milieu,
may you be guided by the ever-present Spirit
and forever live in the abundance of Life!

Contents

Acknowledgments

I would like to acknowledge the vast community of people who have supported this work, starting with my family. To my parents, who are the living example and embodiment of the truth that in and through love all things can be reconciled. Dad, thanks for reading an early edition of this and providing your critical and generous feedback. May the legacy of interracial and intercultural love, starting with you and Mom, be continued through this work. To my multiracial siblings—Alyssa Simonson and Annalisa Poole, who put life on pause to care for me while I was recovering from a severe auto accident during the core writing of this book, you are an eternal treasure.

I am also grateful for the support of Claremont School of Theology and my dear colleagues—Dr. Frank Rogers Jr., Rev. Dr. Nicholas Grier, Rev. Dr. Sheryl Kujawa-Holbrook, Dr. Yohana Junker, Dr. Sharon Jacob, and Dr. Andrew Dreitcer—for your continual and constant support. Your grace, grit, and commitment to a world where all people flourish has profoundly encouraged me as a scholar and fellow human being. Thank you for continuing to help me to trust my own voice and speak it in solidarity with the joy and suffering of the world.

To the Hispanic Theological Initiative for your affirmations, care, and passion. Whether it was an all-expense-paid writing week or an early-career professional development conference, I felt guided by the importance of not doing anything alone! I am immensely thankful for the leadership of Rev. Joanne Rodríguez and the community of scholars who took time to listen to this work, in particular the editing expertise of Dr. Catherine R. Osborne while my research was still in the formative stages, and continue to pray for its success!

To the Disciples Seminary Foundation and the Christian Church (Disciples of Christ) for offering financial assistance, mentorship, and opportunities to ground my scholarship in real-life ministry, I extend my heartfelt gratitude. I am excited to see how the vision of a shared table, where all are included, evokes creative healing in a polarized world.

And finally, thank you to the Vivarium Foundation, beginning with the president, Milena Carrara Pavan, who has offered herself to the promotion and extension of Raimon Panikkar's legacy in the world today. My appreciation goes to the entire jury of readers in the 2022 Raimon Panikkar Prize competition: Young-Chan Ro, Ursula King, Robert Ellsberg, Jaume Agusti Cullel, Peter Phan, Gerard Hall, and Michiko Yusa, who engaged this work and have supported its publication with Orbis Books. I am so happy that this work has been so carefully engaged by Rev. Dr. Thomas Hermans-Webster, whose editorial and publication skills were invaluable in bringing this book to completion. Lastly, thank you, Raimon Panikkar. May this book invite others to know personally the Cosmotheandric Experience. And so it is.

Introduction

An Invitation to Multi/racial Experience(s)

To begin, I offer an entry from my journal reflecting on my own experience of multiraciality.

> I have spent the last decade of my life in institutions dominated by the histories and forces of white supremacy and racism, enduring multiple first-hand experiences of systemic racial oppression.[1] At times I have felt exhausted and at other times suffocated by repeated events of dismissal, scapegoating, and exile from participation in the life of community. As a cisgender, heterosexual, mixed-race man of color who is both Chinese-Malaysian and Mexican-American, I recognize the many ways I am tempted to reduce my experience to only an aspect of me. Yet, despite this

1. As a double-minority, mixed-race man of color growing up in many predominantly white spaces, I have experienced significant social and psychological distress due to racism throughout my entire lifetime. However, despite this, I also acknowledge there is more to my existence than experiences of racialization. I was blessed to have a close-knit immediate family with parents and siblings who loved and encouraged me. These experiences laid a foundation for my understanding of spirituality as both adventure and resistance. It is these same communal and internal resources that renew me as I continue to navigate the deadly terrain of racism prevalent in the United States of America.

pressure, I have found ways to integrate my experiences of contemplative practices and spiritualities, guided by wonderful spiritual teachers and role models, helping me to recover and reclaim the fullness of Being. Following their witness, I have received empowering mystical insights, revealing my own inherent goodness, worth, and value despite the oppression I have faced.

These realizations have compelled me to continue the work of healing justice, even in moments that involve risk to my finances, psychological well-being, and social community. I have come to realize, in moments of direct mystical experience with the divine, that compassion is the primordial energetic force of the world and is potent to transform the hatred, fear, and evil that run rampant in our world.

It has been through spirituality that I have found both safety and healing, as well as the inspiration to embody courageous action in racialized situations. While spirituality can be a way to escape from suffering as a form of bypassing, I have also found that spirituality can offer endless resources to confront, resist, and transform various manifestations of racial oppression. Through spiritual practice, my imagination has been renewed, and I have been charged to bear witness to that within the human experience which race/racism can never tarnish, namely, the possibility of healing together.

I therefore see the potentiality for spirituality to be a vital resource of empowerment and resistance for those struggling to overcome forces of racism in their own lives and in society. More specifically, to those who are multiracial, mystical expansiveness can be a potential

> path enabling others to hold opposites within themselves and provide reconnection in situations of feeling isolated or alone. In my life, I have been granted the gift of recovery of my own inner resources that I had forgotten and a reclamation of the value of my own voice (and the cultures from which I hail) in the path toward liberation. I continue to become aware of both my own temporality and also the mysterious limitless Spirit that moves within (and as) my very life. This path affirms our inherent dignity and personhood and is sustained in the communal presence of one another (or as we say in my background, *en conjunto*). I do not just hope this is true; it is something I have personally tasted and is what I long to invite others to experience. It is with anticipation and hope that I begin the process of being liberated from racial oppression even while fully acknowledging the impacts of race in our midst, first in talking about it truthfully and secondly, to transcend its oppressive power by no longer allowing racial rules and assumptions to silence my voice. But this is not just about my voice, it is about all voices that have been silenced or victimized. The time is now to rise up and say another way is possible.—*Aizaiah Yong,* journal entry, Los Angeles, CA, 2019

I have chosen to begin each chapter with a short journal entry as core to my practical theological method demonstrating the ways in which I personally am implicated into this research as well as to emphasize the importance of each of us in the work of healing justice. In addition, each entry incarnates my conviction that my purpose in writing aligns with my commitment to contemplative practice and living an anchored life. It is through many kinds of practices of contemplation (such as writing) that

I find sustenance and resourcing to engage the world. Furthermore, this commitment assumes that the journey one takes to do anything is just as significant, if not more so, as whatever the outcome. As we continue to live through an increasingly polarized, isolated, and accelerated age, this book intends to *contemplate*[2] the rich and diverse experiences of multiracial people and share the wisdoms they embody as a practical theology of multiraciality so that the world might move toward greater wholeness and transformation. By way of further introduction, the first half of this chapter will be focused on raising the important questions, realities, and ideas that foreground this book. In the second half, I discuss the focus of the book along with my methodological approach.

A Book of Multiraciality

In a book dedicated to addressing the flourishing of people in North America, one must first have a keen understanding of race and racism. In practical theology, it is common for practical theologians to turn to disciplines outside of theology to begin.[3] Racism (and the category of "race" that was created in its support) is well known as a modern Western historical and socio-political project that has wedded itself to the Christian religion,[4] creating theologies that justify the construction of the modern colonial empire by the economic exploitation of nonwhite and poor

2. I generally use *italics* to signal a verb that I am actively participating in and to which I also invite the reader. On occasion, I use it adjectivally to emphasize a particular way of viewing a concept or idea.

3. Don Browning, *A Fundamental Practical Theology: Descriptive and Strategic Proposals* (Minneapolis: Fortress Press, 1991).

4. Willie Jennings, *The Christian Imagination: Theology and the Origins of Race* (New Haven, CT: Yale University Press, 2010).

people.[5] Since the creation of race in the early modern period, racist ideologies and cultures have been exported through colonialism and its various enterprises in countless ways around the world and continue to wreak social and psychospiritual devastation upon all people, not least Black, Indigenous, and People of Color (BIPOC) communities in the United States of America. This is not to deny that ethnocentrisms abound even across non-Western cultural regions of the world going back centuries.[6] But, it is to say that the European construct with its legacy in North America is what I am focused on in this volume. Today, North American scholars from across disciplines[7] and fields consider racism to be the toxic sludge (and original sin) poisoning the water at the table from which all drink, requiring that any liberating vision of humanity must be cognizant of issues of race and racism.

One such way to understand race and racism is through critical race theory (CRT). CRT is a prominent field of inquiry that began in critical legal studies through the works of Derrick Bell and Kimberlé Crenshaw. CRT has expanded beyond its original field of critical legal studies and is engaged in many other disciplines seeking to analyze how race and racism pervade US life so that possibilities of transformative response can be imagined. CRT asserts that racism is endemic to US society and, therefore, justice cannot be realized without confronting race

5. J. Kameron Carter, *Race: A Theological Account* (New York: Oxford University Press, 2008).

6. Love Sechrest, Johnny Ramírez-Johnson, and Amos Yong, eds., *Can "White" People Be Saved? Triangulating Race, Theology, and Mission* (Westmont, IL: IVP Academic, 2018).

7. See Frank Rogers Jr., "The Way of Radical Compassion" (Lecture, TSF 4097, Claremont School of Theology, 2018); Jim Wallis, *America's Original Sin: Racism, White Privilege, and the Bridge to a New America* (Grand Rapids, MI: Baker, 2017); and Ta-Nehisi Coates, *Between the World and Me* (New York: Random House, 2015).

and racism.[8] Furthermore, one of the most important contributions of CRT is the concept of intersectionality, which demonstrates how social oppression is multiplied differently based on a person's varying social locations and positionalities.[9] CRT has since expanded significantly to focus on different racial/ethnic groups, and new subfields have emerged such as TribalCrit, AsianCrit, LatCrit, and MultiCrit.[10] MultiCrit is the particular lens that centers on the lives of multiracial, or mixed race, people.[11] The work of MultiCrit has since been expanded due to forces of globalization and migration, where researchers from all over the world are acknowledging the growth of mixed-race people and, in response, are dedicating more time and energy to study "mixed-race" populations and how their experiences inform understandings of race and racism at large.[12]

In the US context, an interdisciplinary field called critical mixed-race studies (CMRS) has emerged and features scholars from across psychology, education, ethnic studies, gender studies, theology, and anthropology to ask critical questions about the ways in which multiracial identity formation takes place and to what end. For CMRS, studying multiraciality is not primarily concerned with individualized identity politics but rather how race and racism function, persist, and are perniciously reinscribed

8. Derrick Bell, Richard Delgado, and Jean Stefancic, *The Derrick Bell Reader* (New York: New York University Press, 2005).

9. Kimberlé Crenshaw, *Demarginalizing the Intersection of Race & Sex: A Black Feminist Critique of Antidiscrimination Doctrine, Feminist Theory, and Antiracist Politics* (London: Routledge, 1989).

10. Jessica Harris, "Toward a Critical Multiracial Theory in Education," *International Journal of Qualitative Studies in Education* 29, no. 6 (2016): 795–813.

11. Kerry Rockquemore, David Brunsma, and Daniel Delgado, "Racing to Theory or Retheorizing Race? Understanding the Struggle to Build a Multiracial Identity Theory," *Journal of Social Issues* 65, no. 1 (2009): 13–34.

12. Rebecca King-O'Riain et al., *Global Mixed Race* (New York: New York University Press, 2014).

through histories and structures of power and how these systems can be resisted.[13] Within higher education, CMRS has gained considerable attention. This attention is likely due to the massive increase of young adults who self-identify as mixed race now that two decades have passed since multiracial status was officially added as a racial designation in the 2000 US census.

Noted mixed-race and education scholar Jessica Harris has written about the deadly ways racism specifically impacts the multiracial young adults enrolled at predominantly white universities and colleges: "[Mixed-race students] did not have much hope for the eradication of racism, monoracism, colorism, and other oppressive experiences and structures they faced on campus."[14] Harris borrows "monoracism" from the work of critical race scholars Marc Johnston and Kevin Nadal, who discuss how multiracial persons are constantly assigned into monoracial groups and how relative privilege is given to those who will assimilate to monoracial logic.[15] Harris's work cuts through the assumption of a black/white binary in critical race work and shows how this pattern renders multi/racial experience(s) (and multiracial people) invisible, maintaining "hegemonic identitarian illogic."[16] Harris's work does not inscribe multiraciality as yet another monolithic category for racial self-identification. Rather, Harris aims to promote new racial solidarities by dis-

13. Celeste Curington. "Rethinking Multiracial Formation in the United States: Toward an Intersectional Approach," *Sociology of Race and Ethnicity* 2, no. 1 (2015): 27–41.

14. Harris, "Toward a Critical Multiracial Theory in Education," 810.

15. Marc Johnston and Kevin Nadal, "Multiracial Microaggressions: Exposing Monoracism in Everyday Life and Clinical Practice," in *Microaggressions and Marginality: Manifestation, Dynamics, and Impact*, ed. D. W. Sue (Hoboken, NJ: John Wiley & Sons. 2010), 123–44.

16. Jessica C. Harris and Z. Nicolazzo, "Navigating the Academic Borderlands as Multiracial and Trans* Faculty Members," *Critical Studies in Education* 61, no. 2 (2020): 229–44.

mantling the many and varied forms of racial hierarchy that have long governed US communal life through socio-racial contracts.[17]

While a significant portion of CMRS literature prioritizes the psychological and interpersonal dynamics that encompass multi/racial experience(s), behavioral scientists[18] have shown how issues of multiraciality have significant impacts on policy-making for those living in predominantly BIPOC communities. According to the 2020 US census, "more people than ever" identify as multiracial,[19] and this population is expected to be a majority by 2050.[20] Given current predictions[21] for continued growth in the multiracial population in the United States and globally, it is vital that social justice efforts take seriously the perspectives of multiracial people through research that acknowledges the rich diversity of multiracial stories, which then can enable better-informed decisions of how racial justice can be pursued practically by reallocating resources.[22]

A Note on Multi/racial Multiplicity

In this book, I use the "/" and the "(s)" when I write about multi/racial experience(s) because I want to emphasize that there is not

17. Charles Mills, *The Racial Contract* (Ithaca, NY: Cornell University Press, 1997).

18. Diana T. Sanchez et al., "How Policies Can Address Multiracial Stigma," *Policy Insights from the Behavioral and Brain Sciences* 7, no. 2 (October 2020): 115–22.

19. Sylvia Foster-Frau, Ted Mellnik, and Adrian Blanco, "Mixed-Race Americans Are Fastest-Growing Racial Group, Census Shows," *Washington Post*, October 8, 2021.

20. Gina Potter. "The Invisibility of Multiracial Students: An Emerging Majority by 2050" (EdD diss., UC San Diego, 2009).

21. Pew Research Center, "Multiracial Americans: Counting America's Population | Pew Research Center," June 11, 2015.

22. Molly McKibbin, *Shades of Gray: Writing the New American Multiracialism* (Lincoln: University of Nebraska Press, 2018).

one definition of experiencing multiraciality.[23] I seek to problematize the dominant monocultural and monoracial approaches prevalent within racial justice discourse and action. For pragmatic and conversational purposes, I follow the lead of mixed-race scholars who attest that the terms "multiracial" and "mixed race" can be used interchangeably as referring to those who have parents of differing monoracial and/or ethnic backgrounds from each other. My goal in writing a book on multiraciality, then, is not the creation of another new monolithic racial identity category. As a practical theologian who is also multiracial, I am interested in ways to better support and attend to the psychological, cultural, and social distresses placed on multi/racial experience(s). I am interested in ways to more fully advocate for the diverse contributions that multiracial people offer collective justice work. As I stress that multiraciality is inherently pluralistic, I hope to pursue a multiplicity of spiritualities and spiritual-care practices that will attend to the multidimensional and fluid nature of multiraciality, including but not limited to the contextual, cultural, spiritual, and material dimensions. I further hope that my pursuit allows for more dynamic, holistic, and collaborative social engagements that resist the insidious forces of racial oppression.

Therefore, for the remainder of this work, I will use the "/" and "(s)" when I am specifically referring to the plurality and intersections present within multiracial lives and will also use the terms multiracial and mixed race[24] interchangeably.

23. The resistance to the multiracial population as a monolithic group continues to be problematized in multiracial scholarship. See Jessica Harris, Becka Lorenz, and Nelson Laird, "Engaging in the Margins: Exploring Differences in Biracial Students' Engagement by Racial Heritage," *Journal of Student Affairs Research and Practice* 55, no. 2 (2018): 137–54.

24. I will only use the hyphen in "mixed-race" when directly referring to critical mixed-race studies, which uses it.

I am convinced that, with the enormity of racial oppression, approaches to healing must be holistic (including intrapersonal, interpersonal, structural, and cosmic), pluralistic (to account for the diversity within multiracial persons), and informed by relationships of solidarity with other marginalized groups as well as the entire cosmos. No one-dimensional perspective will suffice.

A Book of Practical Theology

While scholars from ethnic studies, gender studies, political sciences, psychology, and education have begun to address various challenges that multiracial people face, I am interested in the additional goal of finding more empowered ways for multiracial people to live. Practical theology explicitly supports the purpose of empowerment, and I agree with John Swinton and Harriet Mowat who attest, "Practical Theology can be understood to be a framework of enquiry that is driven by the desire to create the circumstances for transformative action that not only seeks after truth and knowledge, but also offers the possibility of radical transformation."[25] Recent practical theologians have made clarion calls for practical theology to address how various social locations impact personal and collective well-being,[26] but multi/racial experience(s) continue to be left out of many of these conversations. As a field, practical theology should be concerned about the political and social ramifications of such exclusions.[27]

25. John Swinton and Harriet Mowat, *Practical Theology and Qualitative Research* (London: SCM, 2016), x.

26. Kathleen A. Cahalan and Gordon S. Mikoski ask for issues of race, ethnicity, gender, class, and sexuality to be prominent in practical theology in *Opening the Field of Practical Theology* (Lanham, MD: Rowman & Littlefield, 2014).

27. Mary Moschella, "Practice Matters: New Directions in Ethnography

HyeRan Kim-Cragg is a practical theologian whose work is a notable example of how the field can pay better attention to multi/racial experience(s). One chapter of her book *Interdependence* is focused on multiracial youth. Kim-Cragg notes how experiences of multiraciality shape one's identity formation in significant ways and, subsequently, how the lives of mixed-race youth and young adults subvert notions of purity and colonial white, heteronormative family. Kim-Cragg's book is significant for practical theology as she builds off the work of James Poling and Donald E. Miller and bears witness to how the sacred is at work outside of the institutional church, transgressing boundaries between the sacred and secular.[28] She seeks to understand the life of the divine by bringing attention to the marginalized experiences of multiraciality, which are marginalized within theological conversations (as investigations on race have long been led by those outside of the institutional church) and from anti-racism work due to monoracial bias. Kim-Cragg affirms that all who are committed to healing from the impacts of colonization would benefit from further investigation of and focus on multi/racial experience(s) as they are integral "learning site[s] of practical theology, linked to the goal of a postcolonial feminist practical theology that stresses the importance of mutual recognition of differences for the sake of the interdependent relationships that God desires."[29]

This book is animated with the desire to enliven and strengthen the interdependent relationships that weave us and

---

and Qualitative Research," in *Pastoral Theology and Care: Critical Trajectories in Theory and Practice*, ed. Jack Ramsay (Hoboken, NJ: John Wiley & Sons, 2018), 8–10.

28. James Poling and Donald E. Miller are known for their advocacy that practical theology be a primary tool toward social justice in *Foundations for a Practical Theology of Ministry* (Nashville, TN: Abingdon Press, 1985).

29. HyeRan Kim-Cragg, *Interdependence: A Postcolonial Feminist Practical Theology* (Eugene, OR: Pickwick Publications, 2018).

all of life together. Throughout the book, I continue to emphasize the need for attention to multiraciality within practical theology. Specifically, I am interested in how racism and racial oppression can be healed and transformed through contemplative spirituality. While turning to spirituality for healing from racism and racial oppression is not new, my concern for multi/racial experience(s) gives the turn a unique depth of meaning. In the next section, I explore how spirituality and spiritual practices have played a prominent role in the formation of those who are committed to racial justice and healing.

The Importance of Spirituality in Social Change

Many North American teachers, mystics, activists, and practical theologians have cultivated healing approaches to issues of race, racism, and racial oppression through their own spiritual formation. Considering the lives of those who have come before, teaching and practicing better ways of living together, is crucial to my argument for a spiritually rooted paradigm shift in our experiences with racism and racial oppression. In this section, I review their examples so as to ground this book in practical theology's long-held conviction that spirituality is a vital component of meaningful social change.

Spiritual luminary, African-American mystic, and advisor to the Rev. Dr. Martin Luther King Jr. during the civil rights movement, Rev. Dr. Howard Thurman believed that the fundamental core of racialized tension was spiritual disillusionment.[30] Thurman believed that, through mysticism and spirituality, a person could recover the power and possibility of healing broken relations within the self and find empowerment to live a

30. Alton Pollard, *Mysticism and Social Change: The Social Witness of Howard Thurman* (New York: P. Lang, 1992).

liberated life amid an oppressive world. Thurman advocates that social violence will only cease when it is first confronted and transformed by engaging the spiritual dimension of each person.[31] Further, Thurman describes Jesus's life teachings as a technique of survival for all those who are oppressed and who have their backs against the wall.[32] The call to liberation by way of spirituality and mysticism demands that both internal and external actions be taken to aid in the recovery and reclamation of cultural and divine resources that have been marginalized for those who have been racially oppressed. In this understanding, spirituality is not just an ethereal individualized experience, but it provides the necessary resources that usher in social transformation and sustained engagement. Furthermore, a person's interior strength is what compels someone to courageously bear witness to love and justice in public, even when it is costly. Thurman's nonviolent and spiritually rooted approach to justice provides a clear rationale for how even the best of social-change efforts hinge on spiritual well-being.[33]

Gloria Anzaldúa is another North American public intellectual and social activist who did not identify as "religious" or "spiritual" but has been vocal about the ways healing from oppression cannot be severed from interiority. She came to her own understanding of spirituality through embracing her own mixed experience. She writes, "It was a foundational change of consciousness that helped me find peace. To be a *mestiza* (mixed) is to operate in pluralistic mode. Nothing is thrust out—the

31. Howard Thurman, *Meditations of the Heart* (Boston: Beacon Press, 1953).

32. Howard Thurman, *Jesus and the Disinherited* (Boston: Beacon Press, 1949), 29.

33. Howard Thurman, *Disciplines of the Spirit* (Richmond, IN: Friends United Press, 1997).

good, the bad, the ugly, nothing rejected, nothing abandoned."[34] Anzaldúa's mystical assessment poignantly reveals how overcoming racialized divisions within is tethered to the interior life and is essential to overcoming social oppression. Though she does not use the language of spirituality, Anzaldúa provides one picture of how one's inner resources enable the person to hold polarities in creative tension and relationship.

In addition to Anzaldúa, other BIPOC and LGBTQIA+ activists from beyond religious traditions have shared similar sentiments in their extensive reflections on the ways that social oppressions, particularly racism, breed through the self's interior distortions of reality.[35] For these activists, experiencing intersecting oppressions (many being Black, women, and queer, and a religious minority within North America)[36] reveals how structural oppressions distort our societal relations with one another and reduce personal loving connections that we have within ourselves as sacred beings. Structural oppressions insidiously limit capacities of healing and sever each of us from the natural wisdom located in our very bodies. These activists and practitioners demonstrate that healing must come through reconnection to what is sacred in all of life. Healthy and necessary connections can only be restored through a renewed spirituality.

In the field of practical theology, Emmanuel Lartey proposes an intercultural spiritual-care paradigm that can attend to the spiritual and holistic needs of racialized bodies in the wake of

34. Gloria Anzaldúa, *Borderlands: The New Mestiza (La frontera)* (San Francisco: Spinsters/Aunt Lute, 1987), 61.

35. Rhonda Magee, *The Inner Work of Racial Justice: Healing Ourselves and Transforming Our Communities through Mindfulness* (New York: TarcherPerigree, 2019).

36. angel Kyodo Williams, Rod Owens, and Jasmine Syedullah, *Radical Dharma: Talking Race, Love, and Liberation* (Berkeley, CA: North Atlantic Books, 2016).

generations of colonization. Lartey makes the case for an intercultural approach by criticizing three other predominant forms of care that are currently being offered: monocultural, cross-cultural, and multicultural.[37] Lartey describes monocultural care as ethnocentric and universalizing. This position assumes there are no true differences among people and prescribes solutions assimilated to the dominant culture. Lartey understands cross-cultural care as that which acknowledges difference when giving care but still assumes a hierarchical position over the "other" when providing care. The goal of cross-cultural care is still to help the person assimilate by subscribing and conforming to the dominant culture. And the third approach is what Lartey calls multicultural care, which understands inherent differences but often oversimplifies and generalizes various social locations as monolithic. Multicultural care thus gives care that is superficial and often unhelpful. In response to these problematic approaches, Lartey proposes a fourth way, what he calls intercultural care. Intercultural care respects the personal processes and unique contexts of the person receiving care and assists people in integrating polarities within their life. Lartey re-imagines an approach to multidimensional spiritual care that respects the pluralistic reality of each person as "like *one* another, like *some* others, and like *no* other."[38] For Lartey, finding healing from social and racial oppression thoroughly involves the spiritual.

For each of these teachers, mystics, activists, and practical theologians, it is imperative that efforts seeking to confront racial oppression within North America be holistic and

37. Emmanuel Lartey, *In Living Color: An Intercultural Approach to Pastoral Care and Counseling* (Philadelphia: Jessica Kingsley Publishers, 2003), 43.

38. This view is not original to Lartey as he borrowed from the work of Clyde Kluckhohn and Henry A. Murray in their book *Personality in Nature, Society, and Culture* (New York: Knopf, 1953).

spiritually resourced. Their descriptions of holistic healing include important aspects of the emotional, social, and material dimensions of life. Yet, while those I have reviewed emphasize the spiritual transformations needed to address race, racism, and social oppression, none have intentionally considered the ramifications of a spiritual approach that tends to multiraciality. In this spirit, this book offers a practical theology committed to addressing race and racial oppression in the world by centering the lived experiences and spiritualities of mixed-race people who are in predominantly white institutions in North America. I ask how understandings of multiraciality change when the spiritual dimensions and realities of multi/racial experience(s) are centered. What are some implications of an emphasis on multiracial people, and how can these implications help address polarization and heal cultural divisions amid racial oppression in North America? I contend that a renewed imagination for healing action in the world today can emerge through attending to the spirituality of multi/racial experience(s).

As I have said above, new prophetic and spiritually grounded paradigms are needed. In North America, the life and thought of the renowned twentieth-century spiritual teacher Raimon Panikkar can provide fertile ground for such a new paradigm. From his own contemplative experiences living betwixt and between the monocultural and monosocial realities imposed on him, Panikkar testified to a new spiritual vision that can enliven anti-racist efforts today. With Panikkar, I am convinced that "no amount of reforms will be able to offer better alternatives unless they are accompanied by and the fruit of a spiritual and personal metanoia."[39]

39. Raimon Panikkar, *The Water of the Drop: Fragments from Panikkar's Diaries*, ed. Milena Carrara Pavan (London: Indian Society for Promoting Christian Knowledge, 2018), 81.

A Book of Contemplation: Introducing Raimon Panikkar as a "Bridge and Prophet" for Multi/racial Experience(s)

Raimon Panikkar Alemany (1918–2010) was a spiritual visionary who lived at the intersections of race, culture, ethnicity, and religion and was famously known as an apostle of interreligious dialogue and intercultural understanding. In the words of Bettina Baeumer, Panikkar was "a bridge and prophet" to a transformation possible at the deepest depths of human experience.[40] Famed scholar of mysticism Ewert Cousins called Panikkar "the greatest global theologian of the twentieth century" because of his openness to embrace his own mixed heritage.[41] While Panikkar was certainly a world-renowned theologian, in this book, I am indebted to Raimon Panikkar as a guide to contemplation. Particularly, Panikkar lived out his unique mysticism in the context of three contemporary realities that are of importance to this book: the underrepresentation of non-Western perspectives in dominant theological and philosophical discourse, the increasing awareness and acceptance of vast cultural diversity in the world, and the central role of mysticism and spirituality in the flourishing of Life.

Panikkar as Subversive Prophet

Raimon Panikkar has been rightfully included along with Thomas Merton, Paul Tillich, and Pope Francis in discussions

40. Bettina Baeumer, Introduction to *Raimundo Panikkar: A Pilgrim across Worlds,* ed. Kapila Vatsyayan and Côme Carpentier de Gourdon (New Delhi: Niyogi Books), 11–16.

41. Ewert Cousins, "Uniting Human, Cosmic and Divine," *America*, January 1, 2007.

of twentieth-century Western spiritual leaders.[42] In addition to his place in such conversations, it is also clear that Panikkar is someone who clearly transcended and transgressed[43] Eurocentric or Western tendencies and must therefore be treated with deep respect for his pluralistic experience.[44] As a critical race theorist,[45] I further assert that, in North America especially, Panikkar has been read more marginally than others, not because of his rich mysticism, his multilingual vernacular, or intellectual magnitude[46] but because he heavily critiqued US individualistic and self-destructive culture.[47] His subversive behavior was evident in his bold embodiment as a Hindu-Catalonian mixed person changing his name from Raimundo to Raimon and Paniker to Panikkar, his insistence in Eurocentric academic spaces "that

42. Fred Dallmayr, *Spiritual Guides: Pathfinders in the Desert* (Notre Dame, IN: University of Notre Dame Press, 2017).

43. Anand Amaladass, "Panikkar's Quest for an Alternative Way of Thinking and Acting," in *Raimon Panikkar: Intercultural and Interreligious Dialogue,* ed. J. Vergés Gifra (Girona: Documenta Universitaria, 2017), 49–69.

44. Michael Barnes, "Neither Myself nor Another—the Interreligious Belonging of Raimon Panikkar," in *Hindu-Christian Dual Belonging,* ed. D. Soars and N. Pohran (London: Routledge, 2022), 49–69.

45. To better understand how I use critical race theory to understand Christianity, white supremacy, and religious nationalism tied to legacies of North American colonization in the US context, see the chapter co-written with Amos Yong entitled "Seeking Healing in an Age of Partisan Division: Reckoning with Theological Education and Resounding the Evangel in the 2020s," in *Faith and Reckoning after Trump,* ed. Miguel De La Torre (Maryknoll, NY: Orbis Books, 2022), 214–27.

46. Peter Phan and Young-Chan Ro center on these qualities of Panikkar in their book *Raimon Panikkar: A Companion to His Life and Thought* (Cambridge: James Clarke, 2018).

47. Panikkar lamented about the status of US society in his journal writing, "Over the past few days I have been struck by seeing the enslavement of the American people and generally of the technological culture . . . I do believe this technological civilization is leading Mankind to suicide" (*The Water of the Drop,* 104).

India had a philosophy!,"[48] and through his reluctance to systematize his thoughts into "dichotomies that the Western talent for classification seems to require in order to clarify every kind of problem."[49] Clearly, Panikkar had deep commitments to "finding an alternative way of thinking . . . against any monocultural claim to universality."[50] It is for these reasons, and through a critical race perspective, that I admire the life and thought of Raimon Panikkar and lift him up as a stark contrast[51] to the predominantly white, Western, and Eurocentric spiritual teachers who have historically been prioritized in North American practical theology.

Panikkar as Intercultural Reconciler

Raimon Panikkar boldly claimed a fourfold religious multiplicity in his own life, recognizing belonging as a Christian, Hindu, Buddhist, and secular person. Furthermore, he recognized the importance of his particular racial/ethnic diversity as the child of a Catalan mother and Indian father.[52] He began the prestigious Gifford Lectures with an acknowledgment of his own mixed-

48. Baeumer, Introduction to *Raimundo Panikkar*, 11.

49. Raimon Panikkar, *Cultures and Religions in Dialogue, Part One: Pluralism and Interculturality*, ed. Milena Carrara Pavan (Maryknoll, NY: Orbis Books, 2018), xvi.

50. Catherine Cornille, "Religious Hybridity and Christian Identity: Promise and Problem," *Currents in Theology and Mission* 48, no. 1 (2021): 283, http://www.currentsjournal.org.

51. Scott Eastham also noted how unfortunate it has been that Raimon Panikkar has not been more widely read (specifically in the English language) because of how important Panikkar's critiques are of Western fundamentalisms including rationalism and scientism and because Eastham believes Panikkar carries "important seeds of renewal the West has forgotten to cultivate" (2013), 24–31.

52. George Gispert-Sauch reflects on how Panikkar asserted his mixed identity, "How often did we hear him to correct people and affirm that he was one hundred percent Indian and one hundred percent Spanish," in *Raimundo*

ness, saying, "I am standing on a podium from which, for an entire century, many great scholars have spoken. I am aware of my responsibility. I happen to be the first Catalan, the first Spaniard, the first Indian, and, with one exception from the Middle East, the first Asian. I feel I should try to convey something of the wisdom of all those countries and continents."[53] He was clear that he embraced his pluralistic racial/ethnic background and that this informed his intercultural theoretical approach[54] and vice versa. In an interview with the *Christian Century*, he shared:

> I was brought up in the Catholic religion by my Spanish mother, but I never stopped trying to be united with the tolerant and generous religion of my father and of my Hindu ancestors. This does not make me a cultural or religious "half-caste," however. Christ was not half man and half God, but fully man and fully God. In the same way, I consider myself 100 percent Hindu and Indian, and 100 percent Catholic and Spanish. How is that possible? By living religion as an experience rather than as an ideology.[55]

Though he does not explicitly engage this theme in his academic writing, Panikkar's radical embrace of his own experi-

---

Panikkar: A Pilgrim across Worlds, ed. Kapila Vatsyayan and Côme Carpentier de Gourdon (New Delhi: Niyogi Books, 2016), 127.

53. Raimon Panikkar, *The Rhythm of Being* (Maryknoll, NY: Orbis Books, 2010), xxv.

54. Oscar Pujol comments on this similarly stating his "karmic circumstances played an important role in his interculturality . . . and was put into practice and incarnated in his life itself"; see "The Intercultural Adventure of the Third Millennium: A Homage to Raimon Panikkar," in *Raimundo Panikkar: A Pilgrim across Worlds*, ed. Kapila Vatsyayan and Côme Carpentier de Gourdon (New Delhi: Niyogi Books, 2016), 191.

55. Raimon Panikkar, "Eruption of Truth: An Interview with Raimon Panikkar," *Christian Century*, August 16–23, 2000: 834.

ence of multiraciality served as the impetus for his interreligious genius. Accordingly, his experience of multiraciality ought to be understood as the implied pretext that undergirds all of his writings and thoughts.

While some have argued that Panikkar's life and writings focused on addressing the "problem between religions,"[56] Panikkar understood his life as participation in *incarnatio continua*,[57] the capacity to both embrace and transform one's culture. For Panikkar, such participation was forged in response to "one of the emerging myths of our time, that of the unity of the human family, seen from the global viewpoint of a culture of Man[58] that embraces all civilizations and religions as many facets, mutually enriching and stimulating."[59] Michiko Yusa describes Panikkar's rich example for a world in turmoil, writing, "Panikkar's urgent concern rested in bringing about a way to a more harmonious and less conflict-laden world sustained by the spirit of reconciliation—which arises out of genuine mutual understanding informed by contemplative wisdom. For Panikkar, engagement

56. Harold Coward, "Panikkar's Approach to Interreligious Dialogue," *Cross Currents* 29, no. 2 (1979): 183–89, https://www.jstor.org/stable/24458014.

57. Phillip Gibbs discusses Panikkar's understanding of *incarnatio continua* as "taking place in a specific cultural milieu and . . . at the same time transforming the culture," in *Dreaming a New Earth: Raimon Panikkar and Indigenous Spiritualities*, ed. Gerard Hall and Joan Hendriks (Preston, Victoria [Australia]: Mosaic Press, 2013), 61.

58. Panikkar used the term "Man" as a way of speaking to the human condition in ways that embraced other than Western understandings, including other languages that he spoke. He was aware of the dangers of patriarchal portrayals of humanity and chose to use the terms he did very intentionally. For more on his rationale in using the term "Man," see *Mysticism and Spirituality, Part Two: Spirituality, the Way of Life* (Maryknoll, NY: Orbis Books, 2014), 283.

59. Raimon Panikkar, *Cultures and Religions in Dialogue, Part Two: Intercultural and Interreligious Dialogue*, ed. Milena Carrara Pavan (Maryknoll, NY: Orbis Books, 2018), xiii.

in intercultural philosophy had the broader aim of giving us a sense of hope for the future of the world."[60] Panikkar's example was both needed and rare. He often felt the struggle that accompanied his reconciliatory posture, writing in his journal, "It is not easy to go against the flow. It takes a lot of humility and a lot of audacity. I live against the flow in everything: the world of Maria G, that of Spain, that of the West, that of India, that of traditional Catholicism, of current agnosticism, of monotheism and atheism, of beliefs and non-beliefs."[61] Panikkar's alternative,[62] counter-cultural, and counter-hegemonic lifestyle resulted in a spirituality that consistently rejected singular or fixed categories of identity and offered an invitation to others to do the same, so they might know themselves more deeply and holistically.

Panikkar's embrace of pluralistic complexity in his own spirituality deepened his intellectual pursuits. Active in diverse conversations and communities, he was able to speak to the heart of contemporary social and spiritual challenges with acuteness while overcoming temptations of binary thinking without also falling into either relativism or syncretism. He rightly understood the impending dangers of "technocratic civilization," which gives rise to supremacist ways of being in the world. In response, he called for the transformation of the world by way of "cultural disarmament, the abandonment of the rut in which modern culture of Western origin has been entrenched: progress, technology, science, democracy, and the world economic

60. Michiko Yusa, "Intercultural Philosophical Wayfaring: An Autobiographical Account in Conversation with a Friend," *Journal of World Philosophies* 3, no. 1 (2018): 128.

61. Panikkar, *The Water of the Drop*, 208.

62. A reference to Amaladass, "Panikkar's Quest for an Alternative Way of Thinking and Acting."

market."[63] Panikkar argued that the healing of the world could only be available through openness, genuine dialogue, relationality, and interculturality—a process of cross-fertilization and mutual fecundation of all beings, including and especially the cosmos itself. He wrote clearly:

> What then is the sociological challenge? It is that in this modern Western society, the system is breaking down. I use this simply as a codeword: the system—that is, the social, political, economic, and religious order—seems to be collapsing. To many people the system seems merely imperfect and unsatisfying. But I dare say that it is unjust and even inhuman. It cannot just be reformed. It has to be redeemed. I called it "technocracy" or "technocentrism." I suggest that this system is falling apart because it has tried to resolve the global human predicament by and with the means and insights of one particular culture or religion.[64]

Panikkar reflected on the cost of trekking a new path that sought to reconcile polarization in the world through interculturality and the archetype of the monk, writing, "a [monk is] universal man; [and] the price of all of this is that he probably ceases to be a normal person."[65] Panikkar's intercultural life can easily be summarized as "ceasing to be a normal person," realizing life as a profoundly mystical and "inter-in-dependent" reality, which he termed The Cosmotheandric Experience.[66]

63. "Cultural Disarmament," Fundació Vivarium Raimon Panikkar, 2022, https://www.raimon-panikkar.org/english/home.html.

64. Panikkar, *Mysticism and Spirituality, Part Two,* 209.

65. Panikkar, *Mysticism and Spirituality, Part Two,* 236.

66. Raimon Panikkar, *Trinitarian and Cosmotheandric Vision*, ed. Milena Carrara Pavan (Maryknoll, NY: Orbis Books, 2019), 165.

Panikkar formed his understanding of the Cosmotheandric Experience through his engagement with philosophy beyond the West, namely *advaita*, living beyond monism or dualism;[67] and it was Panikkar's a-dualistic posture toward life that grounded his stance toward pluralism, impassioning him to call others to delight in the world's diversity.

In my reading, Panikkar cannot be understood through any single category of analysis. He invited the world beyond one-category thinking, spoke across multiple languages, philosophized across disparate academic disciplines, moved intercontinentally across the world, and practiced the monastic life across diverse cultural and religious communities. The "border-crossing mysticism"[68] of his life eventually led him to achieve his ultimate desire of living "at home in the East and West,"[69] wherever he found himself, realizing his identity in Divine Mystery alone.

Panikkar as Interreligious Mystic

The "indispensable hermeneutical key" to understanding Panikkar's life and thought is mysticism and spirituality.[70] Remarking on Panikkar's multivolume *Opera Omnia*, Sante Bagnoli observes that beginning "with the volume on Mysticism is somehow symbolic, because it shows Panikkar's striving to pass on his own experience through his writings, and 'mysticism is the full experience for a man.'" For Bagnoli, rooting Panik-

67. Maria Viswas, "Understanding Advaita: A Panikkarean Perspective for a Cross Cultural Journey," *Tattva Journal of Philosophy* 13, no. 1 (2021): 77–91.

68. Barnes, "Neither Myself nor Another," 33.

69. Panikkar, *Mysticism and Spirituality, Part Two*, 149.

70. Panikkar, *Mysticism and Spirituality, Part Two,* xvii.

kar's writing in mysticism and spirituality is significant to "not merely stimulate further studies but experience" itself.[71]

Panikkar was well aware of the challenges associated with the terms, "mysticism" and "spirituality," and he described how they have been wrongly understood as "esoteric phenomena" and "as separate from . . . the body."[72] He believed that he could offer the needed corrective by living it first and writing about it second. Speaking of mysticism in his personal journal, Panikkar described it as "undoubtedly my way."[73] In his scholarship, he described it as the "supreme experience of Life,"[74] the epitome of human fulfillment. Panikkar used other words as synonyms for *Life* from across wisdom traditions, such as *Being* or *Reality*, building on the wisdom teachings of the Dao from Lao Tzu and Qi from Confucian wisdom. In this book, I resonate with the word (and capitalization) of *Life* because it brings to bear the ways in which the sacred is in and of itself the gift of Life. The gift of Life is given and happening as the present moment and may also be understood as the subject-object relations that characterize the depth dimension of human experience throughout all space and time.

In a practical sense, Panikkar saw mysticism as his greatest contribution to alleviate the suffering of others. When Panikkar gave his rationale for his preference for mysticism he wrote, "If social revolution were the only way to help my fellow-beings to live a more human life, I should simply become an activist revolutionary; if proclaiming the Good News of salvation were the

71. "Opera Omnia Presentation," Fundacio Vivarium Raimon Panikkar, 2022, https://www.raimon-panikkar.org/english/home.html.

72. Panikkar, *Mysticism and Spirituality, Part Two,* xvii.

73. Panikkar, *The Water of the Drop,* 30.

74. Raimon Panikkar, *Mysticism and Spirituality, Part One: Mysticism, the Fullness of Life*, ed. Milena Carrara Pavan (Maryknoll, NY: Orbis Books, 2014), xiii.

solution, I should become a preacher. I think that in this article I justify my Cosmotheandric vocation, which I try to live the best I can—in spite of my conscious and unconscious failings."[75] Panikkar's Cosmotheandric vocation was his personal mysticism, which he hoped to offer others. In spite of his passion for this, he openly taught that there can be no one definitive mysticism that triumphs over the rest. Instead, he focused on carving his own unique path led by his understanding of the mysticism of Jesus Christ, which he also called the "Cosmovision of Christ."[76] In his identification with Christianity, he coined the term *Christophany* to explain his own transformational mystical experience as radically trinitarian, *advaitic*, and interrelational, in harmony with the *Cosmotheandric Principle.* For our discussion, I will delve into detail about these terms in the third chapter.

Panikkar knew the Cosmotheandric experience could not be adequately expressed as a reality separate from mundane experience, as esoteric or exclusive to a few particular people in one culture. Rather, Cosmotheandric experience is the experience of being most fully human, and it is available in differing ways to all people, regardless of life circumstance,[77] across cultures,[78] and in Life's each and every "tempiternal"[79] moment. Milena Carrara Pavan writes that, for Panikkar, "the mystical experi-

75. Panikkar, *The Water of the Drop*, 324.

76. Cynthia Bourgeault, "Christophany Notes by Raimon Panikkar," Contemplative Community, March 12, 2007, https://www.contemplative.org/wp-content/uploads/2009/10/Christophany-Overview.pdf.

77. Panikkar wrote in his journal, "The fullness of life can be realized in any given human condition (in spite of injustices, poverty, etc.)" (*The Water of the Drop*, 51).

78. Panikkar, *Mysticism and Spirituality, Part Two*, 153.

79. One way to describe tempiternity can be found in Panikkar's journal entry as the "experience [of] the uniqueness of each moment. This is immortality" (*The Water of the Drop*, 73).

ence is not a specialization, it is open to all mankind. Every man is a mystic to the extent in which he is aware of the life which flows within him: his greatness lies in this awareness."[80]

Because mysticism is the supreme experience and oneness with Life itself, the wisdom that emerges from this experience is a peculiar liberation from the superficial distractions that often preoccupy and subordinate humanity to ignorance and fear.[81] The liberated mystic receives the gifts of *sat* (being), *cit* (consciousness), and *ananda* (bliss), and, in this triadic structure of consciousness, participates in the flourishing of Life even amid adverse circumstances.[82] No agenda or a priori actions can be pre-determined; rather, the mystic acts spontaneously in respect to the dynamic and ever-flowing harmonious celebration of Life itself. Only the person living in mystical awareness is truly "saved" and able to contribute to actions in connection with "the fullness of Life itself." Such a person has the best opportunity to forgo participation in oppressive behaviors and actions as they are free from the bondages of self-interest. In other words, when people realize that their being is interconnected with all other forms of life (human and nonhuman), they are moved to support the totality of Life (along with their own) rather than destroy it. As a person opens to this experience, their consciousness, passions, desires, ambitions, or impulses that stem from self-survival are transformed in and through connections with the whole of Life.[83]

80. Milena Carrara Pavan, introduction in *Fullness of Life,* ed. K. Acharaya, M. C. Pavan, and W. Parker (Mumbai: Somaiya Publications, 2008), xviii.

81. As Panikkar noted, "What do I experience in being free? First, I have to experience that I am free from fear; that is the prerequisite," in *Mysticism and Spirituality, Part Two,* 327.

82. Panikkar, *Mysticism and Spirituality, Part One,* xiv–xvii.

83. Panikkar, *Cultures and Religions in Dialogue, Part One,* 141.

For Panikkar, spirituality or spiritual practice serves as a "navigation chart" that can lead a person to the transformative realization of interconnected being. A person, then, receives mystical awareness through spiritual practices that foster a foundation of receptivity to all of life and its inter-in-dependencies. Panikkar himself relied on many practices, which he shared with others, but the fruit of these practices was the same: empowering others to be co-participants in what he referred to as the "banquet of life" taking place within (and as) each and every moment.[84] His practices reveal his own role as a spiritual guide.

In this book, I argue that Panikkar is an exemplary guide for multiracial people to imagine new and emergent spiritualities as we navigate racialization and racial oppression. As Bettina Baeumer reflects, "Panikkar could create a bridge also between mysticism and the practical implications of his experience and thought which are very relevant in the present world—the questions of peace, human rights, ecology, all of which cannot be solved without an intercultural and interreligious approach."[85] Panikkar's writings model a willingness to reconcile multiplicity both internally (which is needed to heal from racial oppression) and externally in a racialized world. I am of Hakka Chinese Malaysian and Mexican American descent, and Panikkar's life is a shining beacon of hope[86] that informs how I navigate difference intrapersonally, interpersonally, interculturally, cosmically, and socially.

84. Panikkar, *The Water of the Drop,* 314.

85. Baeumer, Introduction to *Raimundo Panikkar,* 13.

86. Interestingly and to my amazement, I believe Panikkar too may have known the possibility his life could be looked to as an example even when he was alive as he recorded in his journal, "I am witnessing the crisis of many people in my generation and also younger ones. I am not saying that I am immune, but I feel as though I somehow have come through the crisis and am able to show the way out. I may be foolish to say this, and I am not so certain, but I think it is true" (*The Water of the Drop*, 49).

In addition to mixed-race individuals such as Panikkar and myself, Panikkarian philosophy can be a powerful and needed corrective to race relations in the United States, allowing for divergent worlds to flow with the harmonious experience of Life. Panikkarian harmony is not about homogeneity or synthesizing all differences into commonality, but about embracing the transformation that occurs as each difference is open to new ways of being in relation to others. A Panikkarian harmony is a pluralism that asks that we embrace difference within and beyond us, as a necessary mystery that allows Life to exist at all.[87] With Panikkar's mystical witness, I wonder if current conversations on race can be transformed and if we might experience the liberation that he attests is possible:

> Only the mystic will survive. I consider that what I have to say, and what I have generally said in the realm of ideas (and I refer to living, praxis-generating ideas) is relevant and important, but I doubt that my personal life, except for a very small circle of friends, is at all interesting, except for the fact that it could be described in a picturesque way. In other words, I am not convinced that the value of my life is translated into words or writings, or even that it has a paradigmatic value for some or provides the necessary background for understanding my ideas. When I get up before dawn and all is quiet around me, including the stars, I am not doing it to "win heaven," accumulate merit or even simply get some work done. I am not doing it for work, but for life; I am doing it so I may live and live as authentically as I can. To live authentically means to be ready to die tomorrow without missing a thing . . . the mys-

87. Barnes, *Neither Myself nor Another*, 34.

> tical dimension becomes imperative, and redemption acquires its true meaning here. Only through a living symbol, and by associating myself with it, can this be possible. The closer I come to the centre, the nearer I will be to liberating power.[88]

Panikkar's interreligious mysticism shows us a picture of one who is fully alive, "living Life for itself and not something else."[89] Rather than living in order to arrive at certain outcomes or achieve finalized solutions to problems, the one who is fully alive is one who acts in the ultimacy of Truth amid life's incompletions and challenges.[90] Living fully alive, the mystic becomes the priest and the prophet who can courageously and nonviolently confront injustice in the world.[91] "By not acknowledging the power of the powerful and by not allowing [themselves] to feel threatened by the power even when life is at stake,"[92] the mystic lives the epitome of a liberated life that is grounded in knowing that all Life is in relationship and fear has no ultimate foundations.

Focus of the Book

This book prioritizes and reflects on a variety of multi/racial experience(s) and seeks to support them with the life, philosophy, and mysticism of Raimon Panikkar and the methods of critical mixed-race studies and practical theology. While the

88. Phan and Ro, eds., *Raimon Panikkar*, 12.

89. Raimon Panikkar and Milena Carrara Pavan, *A Pilgrimage to Kailash* (New Delhi: Motilal Banarsidass Publishers, 2018), 132.

90. Barnes, *Neither Myself nor Another*.

91. Walter Wink, *Jesus and Nonviolence: A Third Way* (Minneapolis, MN: Fortress Press, 2003).

92. Raimon Panikkar, *A Dwelling Place for Wisdom* (Louisville, KY: Westminster/John Knox Press, 1993), 26.

world continues to weather an onslaught of multiple crises, there is a great need for spiritually rooted contemplation and action. This book is one such attempt to cross-fertilize Panikkarian thought with the rich insights of practical theology for the purposes of healing, transformation, and reconciliation. The purpose of this work is twofold: (1) to support the flourishing of multiracial people holistically, and (2) to pave contemporary paths in North America for broader engagement with Panikkar's life and philosophical contributions for the purposes of peace and justice amid the multiple crises in our world.

As a contemplative practitioner myself, I am deeply inspired by Panikkar's "archetype of the monk" because it seems Panikkar's embrace of monkhood was an important way that he as a mixed-race person found his peculiarity connected to the universal. I wonder how a Panikkarian vision of the monk can invite deeper connection to the depth dimension of Life for multiracial persons who are grappling with the struggle for liberation. The questions that guided this study were:

- What kinds of spiritualities are currently present within multi/racial experience(s)?
- How does our understanding of spirituality change when centering the lives of mixed-race people?
- How can practical theology strengthen its commitments to the flourishing of life as a whole by starting with multiracial people?

My intention is to prioritize multiracial people in these questions and wrestle with their experiences as they uniquely bear witness to the fullness of life by honoring the sacredness of their own body, embracing their full selves and all the identities included, and the plurality of their stories. Through this book, I hope that others who find themselves excluded from monoracial or monocultural settings will also discover ways to experience spiritual wholeness even amid racism and be encouraged to take bold action that is grounded in their sociocultural location and that confronts racial oppression in their local context and in the world. This book is written first as a resource for those engaging the struggle against racial oppression and second to bear witness to a living hope that sustains and animates a sacred response to suffering.

A Triadic (Contemplative) Method

This book privileges an interdisciplinary practical theological method that is triadic in structure and movement.[93] I am at once a practical theologian, a critical-race theorist, and a contemplative. All three of these disciplines are central to the writing of this book, and I weave in and out of each, resisting linear or rationalistically dominated argument, opening myself up to a synthesis that would not be possible if the disciplines were kept isolated and separate. The triadic hermeneutic is a unique method and deserves a brief introductory reflection.

Throughout this study, I depend on a thoroughly practical theological approach that is both traditional and novel. The traditional practical theological method I primarily rely on is "pastoral ethnography" with the intention of honoring the voices and diverse experiences of mixed-race people, increasing their sense of agency amid social oppression.[94] This traditional approach includes interviews, coded analysis of interviewee's written

93. See Joseph Prabhu's discussion on Panikkar's understanding of the trinitarian perichoresis articulating four aspects of reality—tripartite structure, differentiated unity, open-ended character, and rhythmic quality—in his foreword to *The Rhythm of Being*, xvii.

94. Moschella, "Practice Matters," 10.

reflections, as well as participatory observation and action.[95] As I have previously stated, I assume that there is inherent diversity within the myriad of multi/racial experience(s), and thus the need for humility, respect, and openness when engaging the issue(s) of multiraciality is essential. With this perspective, I do not assume any universal definitions of what it means to be multiracial even while I do seek to find themes that may trend across their diversity in order to find previously hidden connections.[96] I make this clarification to reiterate that, although I am discussing multiraciality at large in this book, I do not seek to construct a universal ideology or spirituality that exhaustively meets all the needs of multiracial people. I do not believe this is possible.

As a critical race theorist, I seek to interrogate and problematize the nuances and complexities of how race functions and co-create alternatives that are in solidarity with experiences from the margins. The depth and breadth inherent to multi/racial experience(s) will help each of us to understand the racialized dimensions of one another (especially in the United States). In this book, I aim to resist generalizations and universal prescriptions for multiracial people as these techniques have often been used for racist ends. By centering often forgotten and/or minimized racial experiences, I attempt to support the collective human experience as we uncover new and helpful ways to heal from the destructive effects of racialization. By engaging

95. I relied upon the work of Elaine Graham, "Is Practical Theology a Form of 'Action Research'?," *International Journal of Practical Theology* 17, no. 1 (January 2013), https://doi.org/10.1515/ijpt-2013–0010, and Helen Cameron, ed., *Talking about God in Practice: Theological Action Research and Practical Theology* (London: SCM Press, 2010), to create my own practical theological methodology.

96. John W. Creswell, *Research Design: Qualitative, Quantitative, and Mixed Methods Approaches*, 3rd ed. (Thousand Oaks, CA: Sage Publications, 2009).

race-talk, I seek to redeem and transform conversations about race to be more robust and inclusive of the many cultures and experiences of multiracial people so that the entire structural (il)logic of race (which includes racisms, monoracism, and racialization) might be rendered defunct altogether. This book does not intend to eradicate race-talk but to transform how we relate to race and racialization through the power of our innermost wisdom.

Finally, this book is written in the spirit of devoted contemplation informed by the life, thought, and mysticism of Raimon Panikkar. As Panikkar wrote, "A book is a drop in the ocean of the public opinion, a sincere prayer is a glass of water, but a book that is the fruit of contemplation can be wholesome rain."[97] Throughout the book, I remain focused with the intention of *advaitic wholesomeness*. This work is grounded in contemplative encounters with Panikkarian mysticism that involve what Scott Eastham has described as a concentric hermeneutical deepening "in, out, and all around." My contemplative approach to this book is inspired by this triad of circles with no clear boundaries or distinctions. I engage practical theology, critical mixed-race studies, and Panikkarian mysticism with a contemplative resistance to academic traditions of separating discourses, people, and experiences from one another. In the first and innermost circle, I give thanks to and for the life and thought of Raimon Panikkar. Here, I have found an example of multiraciality lived out through spirituality, and, as such, his "nine rules"[98] have

97. Panikkar, *The Water of the Drop*, 206.

98. When Panikkar was asked how to best practice contemplation, he responded in typical Panikkar fashion by sharing there is no one "best way" and must include a variety of approaches, yet he had nine rules that rooted him nevertheless. These nine rules have greatly influenced my own approach to integrative diverse spiritual practices in a spirit of contemplation. To read the list, see Panikkar, *A Dwelling Place for Wisdom*, 156.

benefitted me. In the second and outer circle, I operate as a trained critical theorist and bring in critical mixed-race studies as a way to pay attention more acutely to the experiences of those who have experienced multiraciality to better identify racism and how it can be dismantled. Finally, in the third and all-around circle, as a practical theologian, it is not acceptable for me to muse about multiraciality without living in touch with the experiences of other mixed-race people and, following their lead, considering how I can offer support and nourishment to them. As a committed practical theologian, this book includes the qualitative analysis of a newly created spiritual formation program that centers multiraciality.

The book as a whole and each chapter within it unfolds through this triadic contemplative process. I begin with a contemplation of multi/racial experience(s) from across the disciplines of psychology, sociology, literature, and education and then bring those insights into dialogue with the life and thought of Raimon Panikkar. In this cross-fertilization, I create a new spiritual formation program with corresponding qualitative analysis. The book concludes with the fruit of my contemplative and triadic process: a practical theology of multiraciality that I call Multiracial Cosmotheandrism.

Outline of Chapters

In this invitation, I have reviewed the focus of my book and shared its foundational themes, ideas, terms, and methods. I conveyed the background of this book, which is the prevalence of race and racial oppression in the North American context as well as the rationale for focusing on mixed-race people. I then introduced Raimon Panikkar as a contemplative example of what being a spiritually rooted[99] "mixed" person might offer so that new and creative possibilities can be embodied amid a fragmented and divided world.

In the chapter that follows this, I introduce the critical discourse that focuses on mixed-race people in the US context and then review several prominent theories from the fields of psychology, education, and sociology that are foundational for contemporary critical mixed-race studies as an emerging interdisciplinary field created by and for multiracial people. I then transition to provide an overall analysis of multiraciality in its gifts and longings by applying critical race theory, practical theology, and contemplation. My hope is that this chapter will provide both a bigger picture and a sense for the multifaceted and diverse challenges faced by multiracial people and will also demonstrate the vast underrepresentation of multiracial voices. In identifying these various dimensions of multi/racial experience(s), I develop a more substantive and holistic approach to tending to the beauty and challenge of being multiracial in North America for the purposes of identifying spiritual pathways that will better support multiracial people to move toward wholeness.

Chapter 2 focuses on contemplating the life of Raimon Panikkar as a spiritual icon for multiraciality. To do this I categorize his life and thought in five ways that I believe have direct connections to the genius and spiritual longings present in multi/racial experience(s). The five sections are (1) Blessed Simplicity: Panikkar's Roots in the Archetype of the Monk, (2) A Life Fully Lived: Raimon Panikkar's Contemplative Mood, (3) Intrareligious Dialogue and a Pilgrimage to Kailash: Panikkar's Unique Spiritual Practices, (4) A Christophanic Example: Rela-

99. Panikkar wrote the following in his journal, "It is necessary to be rooted and my roots are very clear; but roots are justified because they allow the tree to grow in all different directions" (*The Water of the Drop*, 76).

tionships that Cultivated Panikkar's Mysticism, (5) Mysticism, Compassion, and Multiraciality (MCAM): Creating a Spiritual Formation Program for Multiracial Christophany. This chapter clarifies how I understand Raimon Panikkar to be a spiritual guide for multiracial people par excellence and advocates that multi/racial experience(s) are fundamentally sacred and worthy of tender attention and care. From these foundations, I formulate a new spiritual formation program that centers multiraciality and seeks to lead participants toward their own experience of Multiracial Christophany.

In Chapter 3, I discuss MCAM, the spiritual formation program I created and led, including an overview of the format of the program, the basic contents of what was shared, and highlights of what I discovered through qualitative analysis of it. The program is unabashedly mystical, pluralistic, and collectivist in its commitments by maintaining an unflinching resolve to center multi/racial experience(s)[100] in their struggle to heal racial oppression in society through spiritual, communal, nonviolent methods.[101] The findings arise from the lived experiences of the program participants, and, therefore, much of the chapter is dedicated to direct quotes from the lived experiences of participants. This chapter uplifts the special role mixed-race people can play in empowered and embodied vulnerable risk-taking that creates possibilities for social wholeness where the outcome cannot be predetermined in advance. The conclusions I draw here set the foundation for what I review in the final chapter as

100. I have begun this work and how I understand multiraciality to be important to healing racial oppression in my article "All Mixed Up: Multi/Racial Liberation and Compassion-Based Activism," *Religions* 11, no. 8 (2020): 402.

101. F. Rogers Jr. details how these factors are vital to social change in a lecture he gave during the class "The Way of Radical Compassion" (2018), CST Lecture, TSF 4097.

a new practical theology of multiraciality, which I call "Multiracial Cosmotheandrism," which reveals unique ways multiracial people can spiritually transform racial justice paradigms.

Chapter 4 is grounded in the spiritual step of *discerning new paths forward* and weaves together the entire book, proposing a practical theology of multiraciality called Multiracial Cosmotheandrism. A practical theology of multiraciality is useful in supporting mixed-race people but can also spark imagination for new action(s) to be taken by individuals as well as institutions to heal from race and racial oppression and dream of a future where all can thrive. I conclude the book with imagining how the world could be renewed if a practical theology of multiraciality was more widely embraced. In closing, I share considerations as to how this work might impact the fields of practical theology, critical mixed-race studies, and Panikkarian studies—perhaps deepening engagement with the complexities of North American life in and through a spirit of *blessed simplicity* and contributing to the healing, resistance, and empowerment of people amid ongoing conditions of racialization.

Contribution of the Book

Corresponding with the practical theology of multiraciality that I have called Multiracial Cosmotheandrism, a profound transformation within myself emerged as a fruit of this triadic hermeneutical process. Multiracial Cosmotheandrism celebrates the lives of mixed-race people in their many gifts and wisdoms with the purposes of supporting all those pursuing justice and liberation. In writing this, I hope the various fields of practical theology, critical mixed-race studies, and Panikkarian studies will benefit from this dialogue that not only happened between different peoples, cultures, and spiritualities, but within the depths of my being.

1

Contemplating Multi/racial Experience(s) in the United States

I often think about the first time I was consciously racialized by another. It was on the basketball court in seventh grade. I remember someone in the crowd yelling out, "Look, it's Yao Ming!" At first, I did not know if this was a compliment (because Yao Ming at the time was a professional basketball player and NBA All-Star) or if the person was just ignorant (not knowing Yao Ming was 7′5″). I was 5′0″ at the time, and I played a different position than Yao. So I asked myself, where is the resemblance? I then realized the person was not offering a compliment about my basketball skills but was stereotyping me racially. As I continued to grow older, every time I was in non-Asian spaces, people would call me racial slurs, making fun of my eyes, and assume I was nerdy and unathletic. However, I could not go to Asia to find refuge either. When I first traveled there at age fifteen, I was treated as an "American" and was told that I could not relate to "true Asian experience." Even while I was betwixt and between in my Asian-ness, I rarely if ever was given the opportunity to identify with my Mexican-American roots (as that is the racial-ethnic identity of my mother). Wherever I seemed to go, I was never accepted in my full person as a Chinese Mexican-American. I always longed for a people I could call my own. When I look back on my childhood and adolescence, I notice that conversations on race were very difficult for me. They always brought up a lot of pain, feelings of exclusion and isolation, and when I look back I can see how much energy I spent to avoid "going there." Constantly feeling like a racial outsider in every group takes its toll on a person. When race was brought up (and it certainly almost always is in the United States), people always were surprised to know that I was mixed. Ignorant, insensitive, and apathetic remarks continued to be aimed at me, and for a long time, these challenges kept me from talking openly and honestly about race. My approach was simply to avoid it and try to forget it. Although I never could, because that is what people would always say and come back to during our relationships. My experience has come full circle, and as an adult, I have found beauty and power in sharing my racialized experience, and my hope is that my sharing might also garner strength and courage in others to more fully accept themselves, see themselves as beloved, and work together with others to resist and overcome racism. Racial oppression need not be the end of our stories; we can do better. Perhaps it begins by simply creating space to pay attention (with loving compassion) to our own hurts and tend to them so that we might be able to do the same with others' hurts, all the while not reducing ourselves or others to anything less than infinite mystery.—*Aizaiah Yong,* journal entry, Los Angeles, CA, 2019

Introduction

In this chapter, I take a long and loving look[1] at multi/racial experience(s) by reviewing histories, psychological theories, and insights coming from education that center multi/racial experience(s). The literature that comes from critical mixed-race studies is part of the "out" movement of my triadic method. This chapter also attests to the diversity of multi/racial experience(s) and seeks to confront these through a depth dimension of interiority, otherwise known as a contemplative spirit.[2] My attempt to engage the critical from a contemplative posture signals the "in" movement of my triadic method.

While this entire chapter is fashioned to celebrate and promote the lives of multiracial people, this process must also include acknowledging the challenges and sufferings they face as well. One without the other would be incomplete and could result in either romanticizing, exoticizing, or patronizing the experiences of others. The intention of this chapter is to invite the reader to gain both knowledge (about) and love[3] (for) multiracial people which will allow for those who are not multiracial to appreciate multi/racial experience(s). As I invite those on the outside of multiraciality to engage with this work, I recall the "all around" movement within my triadic method. In this spirit,

1. A term borrowed from Walter J. Burghardt in "Contemplation: A Long Loving Look at the Real," *Church*, no. 5 (Winter 1989): 10.

2. See Panikkar's full treatment of contemplation as an act of ultimate importance in the world in *Mysticism and Spirituality, Part One: Mysticism, the Fullness of Life*, ed. Milena Carrara Pavan (Maryknoll, NY: Orbis Books, 2014), 43–44.

3. Panikkar discussed the union between knowledge and love as *prajna-karuna-mithuna* (translated from Mahayana Buddhism as knowledge, compassion, and matrimony) and is the "hope for humankind" in *Cultures and Religions in Dialogue, Part One: Pluralism and Interculturality*, ed. Milena Carrara Pavan (Maryknoll, NY: Orbis Books, 2018), 204–50.

I intend to reclaim the hidden wisdoms present in multi/racial experience(s) with the ultimate aim of furthering efforts that tend to the spiritualities of mixed-race people and that promote collective solidarity and interconnectedness. In the final section of this chapter, I define four spiritual themes that emanate from multi/racial experience(s) that are essential to address when supporting multiracial flourishing.

Multiplicity in Multiraciality: Reviewing the Diversity of Multi/racial Experience(s)

Critical Mixed-Race Studies (CMRS)

An exciting and burgeoning conversation in critical race scholarship in recent years has been the development of a new interdisciplinary field called critical mixed-race studies (CMRS). A group of scholars began working on the new field in 2013 at the University of California-Berkeley as a direct response to conservative politicians and their attempts to coopt multiracial political advocacy efforts and pit them against other racial groups who were pursuing racial justice. CMRS responded to these efforts by affirming the importance of race consciousness (particularly in the lives of mixed-race people) and calling attention to the many ways mixed-race people can act in solidarity with others for racial justice. CMRS scholars were motivated by the misinterpretation of their activism and reiterated how their work was not an attempt to disregard anti-racist efforts but instead to more deeply engage them.

CMRS accomplished this engagement in two significant ways. First, they acknowledged the history of "passing" and colorism within multi/racial experience(s), including the preferential treatment of light-skinned people due to proximity to whiteness during and following slavery. Second, they demonstrated how mixed-race people can uniquely strengthen racial justice by analyzing histories of forgetfulness and erasure, organizing for political action, and encouraging agency and self-determination. From early in their work, CMRS scholars were clear in their goals: to combat racism in every form and to partner with other racial activist groups such as the Chicano movement and the Asian/Pacific Islander model minority movement. The CMRS scholars repeatedly insisted that they were not seeking proximity to whiteness or to reassert a new racial hierarchy with a monolithic multiracial identity, but instead that they desired to denounce any and all forms of racism and racial oppression that impact society, starting with the unique impacts upon multiracial people. G. Reginald Daniel specifically highlights the critical mass of those who identify as multiracial and the population's potential impacts to address the realities of race, racism, and white supremacy anew.[4] CMRS also seeks to broaden and diversify the multiracial conversation beyond those who are mixed with white and nonwhite parents, on whom much of the research up to this point has focused.[5] From the inception of CMRS, the work has maintained an activist edge and is aided by a gamut of often disparate academic fields.

The short history of CMRS indicates that literature on multi/racial experience(s) are still vastly underrepresented and underdeveloped. To avoid lumping all multi/racial experience(s) together, CMRS continues to be an interdisciplinary field, embracing perspectives from history, psychology, education, and sociology

4. G. Reginald Daniel (2021) names these three objectives as what holds CMRS together.

5. Jayne Ifekwunigwe, ed., *"Mixed Race" Studies: A Reader* (New York: Routledge, 2004); Lauren Davenport, *Politics beyond Black and White: Biracial Identity and Attitudes in America* (Cambridge: Cambridge University Press, 2018).

to paint a fuller picture of the dynamic scope of multi/racial experience(s). While CMRS has emerged from the insights of many fields, four are significant for this chapter. Mixed-race histories allow for a deeper analysis of how power was used institutionally and structurally for the purposes of racism and colonization. Mixed-race psychology emphasizes the importance of how race is experienced and interpreted at individual levels. Multiraciality in higher education depicts the environment within which the largest number of self-identified multiracial people currently exist. And from a sociological lens, MultiCrit stems from a deep engagement and adaption with critical race theory.

Multiracial Histories

In the year 2000, the US census for the first time allowed persons to check more than one race when selecting their racial identity. Yet racial mixing has a much longer history than formal census recognition. Racial mixing, also known in US history and law as miscegenation, is a phenomenon that can be traced to colonial conquests. Typically, European men had sexual relations with Indigenous or African women who were brought through the trans-Atlantic slave trade to the United States, and the women were then victims of sexual violence, causing them to bear multiracial children.

In the United States, a system colloquially known as the "one-drop rule" relegated people with any ancestry outside of "white" racial status to an inferior "nonwhite" position regardless of the person's appearance. These structures denied multiracial children the societal benefits of their white ancestry and paralleled systems of racial hierarchy in other countries. Davenport draws connections between the US system of "hypodescent," the Brazilian *pardo* system, and the South African designation of multiracial people as *coloured* and marginalized from those who are considered "racially pure." Political minoritization is at the heart of all these systems.[6]

Although interracial union has been present since the beginning of the United States, it was only in 1967 that laws against interracial marriage were completely abolished throughout the country. And it was not until even more recently, in the 2000s, that interracial marriages gained popular approval in US society.[7] The increase in popular approval of interracial relationships could be understood due to two primary factors: (1) a proliferation of interracial marriages (predominantly in California) and (2) a growing number of those who identified as "two or more races" on the 2010 census. Between the 2000 and the 2010 census, the number of people identifying as multiracial grew by 33 percent. Yet, mixed-race people still face the onslaught of racism in their everyday lives. Thus, even while popular media often romanticize interracial couples and multi/racial experience(s), claiming that these persons represent a post-racial society, in their caricature, they fail to address how racism has now disguised itself differently in the lives of multiracial people.

Reflecting on mixed-race histories in the United States reveals how race has been and is politically and socially constructed rather than biologically immutable. Furthermore, these constructions bear immense implications for one's opportunities and experiences of privilege in a given society.

Multiracial Psychologies

While multiracial histories have made important contributions to understanding and analyzing societal legacies of racial

6. Davenport, *Politics beyond Black and White.*
7. Davenport, *Politics beyond Black and White.*

constructs, multiracial psychology has worked to assist multiracial people in their individual processes of self-identification and self-determination. Carlos Poston and Kristen Renn are two multiracial psychologists who have each developed theories for multiracial identity formation. Poston's work normalizes the need for spaciousness in supporting a mixed-race person's psychological development through five stages: personal identity based on one's personality from the original family system, choice group categorization that attends to a person's forced choosing due to social factors, enmeshment or denial that is characterized by guilt or self-hatred for aspects of their mixedness, appreciation as an openness to exploring one's multiplicity, and integration by experiencing wholeness and creative connections amid plurality. In Poston's model, multiracial people may grow more comfortable with identifying with the multiple aspects of their racial heritage, and it is possible for people to grow into integration. In the stage of integration, people are invited to accept themselves fully without having to consider their experience inferior to monoracial people. Additionally, they would be able to draw upon their multiple backgrounds for their own enrichment and flourishing. Poston likens integration to holding multiple racial and cultural realities at once and shows how this capacity significantly decreases the reality of polarization within the self.[8]

Renn created an "ecological model," which places high importance on the context of the person's life to discern the best responses for how multiracial people will respond to any given moment. For Renn, the most important factors that impact how multiracial people choose to engage race and racialization are contextual, including physical appearance, cultural knowledge,

8. Carlos Poston, "The Biracial Identity Development Model: A Needed Addition," *Journal of Counseling & Development* 69, no. 2 (1990): 152–55.

and peer culture.[9] In her model, Renn notes that responses can vary from monoraciality to multiple monoraciality, multiraciality, extraraciality, or situational raciality. She further emphasizes that each multiracial person will act in response to numerous contextual factors that change case by case.

The models share an assumption that a multiracial person is largely excluded from prevailing monoracial paradigms. Similar to the findings of Sarah Townsend et al.,[10] even when a multiracial person identifies with a particular monoracial paradigm, their identification comes with a cost and must overcome the consistent denial from others with regard to their racialized experiences. Both Poston and Renn affirm the inherent relationality of race and the necessity for a mixed-race person to navigate multiple relations simultaneously. The mixed-race person's capacity to embrace distinct pluralistic racial identities in a variety of settings is paramount to the person's psychological well-being. Research has proven that multiracial people are at risk for mental-health issues because of the constant social pressure to identify monoracially, and disregard integral aspects to their own understanding of racialization.[11] It is therefore evident that, due to the highly subjective realities of multiraciality, healing or the lack thereof is predicated on the presence of others.

In review, multiracial psychology argues that multiracial people have a diversity of distinct, racialized experiences such as

9. Kristen Renn, "Research on Biracial and Multiracial Identity Development: Overview and Synthesis," *New Directions for Student Services* (2008): 13–21.

10. Sarah S. M. Townsend, Hazel R. Markus, and Hilary B. Bergsieker, "My Choice, Your Categories: The Denial of Multiracial Identities," *Journal of Social Issues* 65, no. 1 (March 2009): 185–204.

11. Margaret Shih and Diana Sanchez, "When Race Becomes Even More Complex: Toward Understanding the Landscape of Multiracial Identity and Experiences," *Journal of Social Issues* 65, no. 1 (2009): 1–11.

life stages, social dynamics, economic conditions, and racialized structures within institutions that must be tended to carefully in order to best support a multiracial person's self-esteem, promote a higher sense of efficacy and empowerment, and lower their vulnerability to stereotypes.[12] Furthermore, a diversity of experiences demands a diversity of new emergent pathways[13] to support mixed-race people toward the goal of multiracial flourishing.

Multiraciality in Higher Education

One of the most popular fields to embrace and significantly contribute to critical mixed-race studies is higher education. Previous studies from within higher education have paved the way for better understanding the imperatives for anti-racist formational work in the lives of young adults in North America. Previous studies have focused on assisting students in identifying color blindness, recognizing implicit bias, and analyzing systems of power, privilege, and oppression. Yet, while each of these areas is important, there has only recently been more attention given to how these formational efforts can serve multiracial people.[14]

12. Renn, "Research on Biracial and Multiracial Identity Development"; K. Pauker, C. Meyers, D. T. Sanchez, S. E. Gaither, and D. M. Young, "A Review of Multiracial Malleability: Identity, Categorization, and Shifting Racial Attitudes," *Social and Personality Psychology Compass* 12, no. 6 (2018).

13. One example of this is the conclusive recommendations that advocate for the need that future research more clearly differentiate between *racial identity* (an individual's self-understanding), *racial identification* (how others understand and categorize an individual), and *racial category* (what racial identities are available and chosen in a specific context) "in order to imagine the most fruitful pathways forward," in Kerry Ann Rockquemore, David L. Brunsma, and Daniel J. Delgado, "Racing to Theory or Retheorizing Race? Understanding the Struggle to Build a Multiracial Identity Theory," *Journal of Social Issues* 65, no. 1 (March 2009): 13–34.

14. Michele Berger and Kathleen Guidroz, eds., *The Intersectional Approach: Transforming the Academy through Race, Class, and Gender* (Chapel Hill: University of North Carolina Press, 2009).

Attending to multiracial histories reveals that the historical absence of mixed-race perspectives, even if unintentionally, stems from structural patterns of monoracism in society. The impacts of exclusion on multiracial people have been well documented and particularly vicious because of invisibility under monoracial paradigms. These cycles of exclusion can be broken by beginning with increased awareness and acceptance of the complexities of multi/racial experience(s).[15] There exists today an ever-growing need for institutional spaces to be created and offered as the mixed-race population in the United States continues to grow into adulthood and is expected to multiply in the coming years.

Scholars of and activists in education have found that multiracial students, staff, faculty, and administration still confront forced options in their racial identification where monoracial paradigms are dominant. Four options are regularly identified. First, multiracial people must accept the single racial identity assigned to them. This assignment varies depending on their racial background. Second, multiracial people must choose a single racial identity for themselves to be part of the conversation at the exclusion of the double nature of their racial heritage. Third, multiracial people must construct an individualized racial identity; for example, a Black and Asian person identifying as "blasian." A fourth option forces multiracial people to choose the race identity of being "'mixed,' 'biracial,' or 'multiracial.'"[16] While multiracial people may be able to identify as a person of color or as white depending on the context, neither of these

15. Marc Guerrero Johnston and Charmaine Wijeyesinghe, eds., *Multiracial Experiences in Higher Education: Contesting Knowledge, Honoring Voice, and Innovating Practice,* 1st ed. (Sterling, VA: Stylus Publishing, 2021).

16. Loretta Winters and Herman DeBose, eds., *New Faces in a Changing America: Multiracial Identity in the 21st Century* (Thousand Oaks, CA: Sage Publications, 2003).

choices allows for the fullness of their racialized experience to be embraced, inadvertently subverting the goal of holistic inclusion through racial justice work. All of the options that multiracial people are currently given reduce multi/racial experience(s) to either being on the outside of a white group or on the outside of identifying completely with people of color. While this is true in one sense, it does not provide much room to understand the nuances of how racism and racial oppression manifest in the lives of mixed-race people. Likewise, it does not give others who are not multiracial any opportunity to deepen understanding of what it is like to be multiracial in the United States.

This repeated pattern leaves multi/racial experience(s) fragmented, excluded, and further minoritized, impacting the most those who are, as Chelsea Guillermo-Wann describes, "double minorities." Furthermore, Guillermo-Wann writes, "When multiracial quantitative data are aggregated as a group, students indicate higher mean levels of discrimination and bias as an aspect of the behavioral dimension than do monoracially classified Latina/o or white students, and double-minority multiracial students indicate higher levels than their peers indicating minority/white multiracial backgrounds."[17] This dilemma often leaves multiracial people excluded and unable to provide input and/or reflection to much-needed critical analysis on various manifestations of institutional and structural racism.

Other efforts within critical race education focus on allowing for plurality in the classroom. Stemming from Paulo Freire's *Pedagogy of the Oppressed* (1970), critical race educator and scholar Rachel Luft emphasizes the need for communities to collectively dismantle racism and white supremacy by starting in their own

17. Chelsea Guillermo-Wann (*Mixed) Race Matters: Racial Theory, Classification, and Campus Climate*, PhD diss., University of California Los Angeles (ProQuest, 2013), 132, http://www.proquest.com.

communities.[18] Luft suggests that this critical race educational work starts at the microlevel of the individual classroom, reviewing the permanence of race and how racism is always at work, before introducing other intersecting identities to the conversation such as gender, class, ability, etc. Finally, when students understand these dynamics, Luft recommends a full intersectional analysis of race where oppressions of religion, language, sexuality, and educational background, among others, intersect and are constantly re-created. Patricia Collins and Sirma Bilge develop critical race educator Bonnie Dill Thornton's insights that "intersectionality is the intellectual core of diversity work" and that those who sit at the intersections of multiple oppressions have an "epistemological edge" on the realities of oppression.[19] Mixed-race scholars and activists have something important to add to this work but will only be able to do so when spaces are created that normalize mixed-race experiences and understand the intra-personal, interpersonal, and structural manifestations of racism that are specifically enacted against multiracial people.

Chelsea Guillermo-Wann lifts up a possible model for including mixed-race people more fully in her work.[20] The Integrative Model of Multiraciality (IMM) incorporates critical race theory, multiracial identity development, campus climate, and racial formation theory to better understand how multiracial students face barriers in schools and how education can better be adapted in light of their experiences to address the many ways in which

18. Rachel E. Luft, "Intersectionality and the Risk of Flattening Difference Gender and Race Logics, and the Strategic Use of Antiracist Singularity," in Berger and Guidroz, eds., *The Intersectional Approach*, 100–117.

19. Patricia Hill Collins and Sirma Bilge, *Intersectionality: Key Concepts* (Chichester: Wiley, 2016), 40.

20. Chelsea Guillermo-Wann, "Integrative Model of Multiraciality (IMM)," *Bi-Annual Critical Mixed Race Studies Conference* (Los Angeles: University of California, 2012), 57.

racism and racial oppression show up. Studies show that multiracial students suffer both from traditional racism(s) that interlock with gender-, class-, and other identity-based oppression, as well as monoracism from the groups with which they share racial heritage. These observations testify to the fact that multi/racial experience(s) have unique vantage points on how racism operates in the United States. Furthermore, these studies can be used to justify the centering of multi/racial experience(s) for coalition building with others who feel marginalized by essentialist racial identity structures. These coalitions may complement organizing efforts across other issue-specific groups that seek to collectively promote social justice such as women's, LGBTQ+, and low-income groups.

MultiCrit

MultiCrit is a paradigm created by Jessica Harris[21] that adapted the tenets of critical race theory[22] to the structural and systematic marginalization of mixed-race people. All CRT tenets are re-emphasized in MultiCrit. I argue that four specific principles[23] can help better support multi/racial experience(s): (1) the *non-neutrality* of law or policies, (2) the recognition of and resistance to *monolithic approaches* in anti-racist efforts, (3) the challenge to the US ideology of *meritocracy,* and (4) the principle of *intersectionality.*[24]

21. Jessica Harris, "Toward a Critical Multiracial Theory in Education," *International Journal of Qualitative Studies in Education* 29, no. 6 (2016): 795–813.

22. Richard Delgado and Jean Stefancic, *Critical Race Theory* (New York: New York University Press, 2005).

23. Richard Delgado and Jean Stefancic, *The Derrick Bell Reader*, Critical America (New York: New York University Press, 2005).

24. Kimberlé Crenshaw, ed., *Critical Race Theory: The Key Writings That Formed the Movement* (New York: New Press, 1995).

MultiCrit claims that North American institutions privilege white supremacist and colonial ways of being that, in turn, disadvantage those who are nonwhite. Harris nuances this point by arguing that it is specifically monoracism and colorism that govern institutional policies and racial justice efforts. Harris's study emphasizes the many ways in which multiracial students experience institutional delegitimization because they do not subscribe to monoracial identities and have no access to groups or community-life funding to support interests and issues that matter to them. According to Harris, racism and white supremacy are built on the assumptions of race as an essentialized difference and essentialized identity. In turn, this essentialist rationale supports the need for racial hierarchy, and it does not create any room for the reality of those who do not fit into the essentialized categories and live in relational ways that transcend clearly delineated boundaries. This is an affirmation of CRT's commitments to anti-essentialism, and Harris supports anti-racist efforts to build connections based on shared experiences of liminality.

Emphasizing the experiences of liminality, MultiCrit also repeatedly rejects monolithic approaches in anti-racist efforts. Harris gives a narrative example of how multiracial people are often categorized differently depending on their context and yet always in ways that support the status quo. Harris tells of one multiracial undergraduate student who shared that a university staff member told her that she was proud of her because the student worked hard, "unlike other people of color" the staffer knew, separating her from other people of color. Immediately after this statement, the staff member asked the student if she would be willing to be featured for marketing purposes to show off the office's diversity. This interaction illustrates the presence of both "color-blind" racial oppression and racist tokenism for this student, ensuring that white normativity is maintained.

Harris calls this experience one of "racial differentialization" and discusses the need for more adaptive, relational, and contextual responses to be taken in these encounters. Furthermore, she advocates for continual imagining and enacting of various approaches of resistance to racism in light of continuously emerging realities.

This example also proves why overcoming racism cannot happen by minimizing, ignoring, or avoiding racialized dynamics, and instead focusing on "other issues." While some liberal proponents argue for patience and hard work as the key to "progress," such arguments can become an easy call to delay justice and minimize the ongoing and felt impacts of racism, creating more excuses for the patterns to continue. According to MultiCrit, these arguments rely on US mythologies of progress and meritocracy that are often used to assume and assimilate to monoracism and monoracial paradigms. Rather than accepting these myths, people who are racially minoritized must find ways of becoming aware of racial dynamics and do something different so that things change. Herein lies the power of MultiCrit, which calls for emergent and nuanced action to be taken.

One of Harris's most important contributions with MultiCrit is the way she describes the challenge of intersectionality for multiracial people. Harris modifies intersectionality for the multiracial person by focusing on three main factors: the marginality of subjectivity, the construction of identity, and the matrix of oppression. Harris recounts the intersectional oppression of those who are mistreated due to belonging to two different racial groups. She shares examples of an Indian Mexican student (Punjabi Mexican) and a Mexican Filipino (who spoke of herself as Mexipino). Both students experienced instances of macro- and microaggressions, as they were classified by members of their own racial groups as "half-breeds or mutts" or as not "true Mexicans." Harris claims that for the wisdom of intersectionality to speak to mixed-race people, it needs to understand multiple minority status within race itself and not seek to reduce or treat people as racial monoliths. The insights found in multiple minority experiences have parallels with others from gender[25] and sexuality[26] studies that understand these identities to be more on a spectrum than anything explicit or set in stone. Harris emphasizes that when multiple minority status is not analyzed, the cost is that multiracial people will be negatively treated for their refusal to identify monoracially or insist on their own multiracial recognition. This kind of exclusion is multiplied by other social categories when people are assigned to them. While multiracial people have a leg up in realizing that categories are not static, they continue to be silenced in their truth-telling. Harris advocates for MultiCrit as a powerful tool of analysis to understand how white supremacy and racial oppression operationalize at the expense and to the detriment of multiracial people. Harris's commitment to ending racial oppression sets the stage for a new spiritual approach to be considered.

Emphasizing the Spiritual Dimensions of Multiraciality: A Contemplative Approach

While CMRS has done well to include multiple mixed-race voices in their literature, it can be significantly aided by the presence of contemplative and spiritual paradigms. This section weaves the insights of multiracial histories, psychology, education, and MultiCrit, bringing them into conversation with contemporary spirituality studies to identify four *spiritual* themes of multi-

25. Judith Butler, *Gender Trouble: Feminism and the Subversion of Identity* (New York: Routledge, 2006).

26. Marcella Althaus-Reid, *The Queer God* (London: Routledge, 2003).

raciality. In doing this, I provide more than a critical assessment of multiraciality, but a *contemplation* of multiraciality, informed by my own contemplative triadic method. My approach seeks to make more apparent the varied wisdoms of multiraciality and better clarify appropriate responses to the destructive impacts from racism and racial oppression. This chapter also demonstrates how I specifically understand challenges to multiraciality to also be spiritual in essence, which further explains my reasoning as to why I believe that any approach seeking to ameliorate racial oppression in the lives of mixed-race people must involve *spiritual dimensions* at its core. I will consider how each spiritual theme offers both the wisdom of multiracial people and also beckons that emergent and innovative spiritualities be created that can more carefully support multiracial people in overcoming what I call *race-based cynicism,* which can result in hopelessness and despair.[27]

The four spiritual themes I have identified within multiraciality include (disregarded) ancestors, (distorted) attitudes, (devitalized) actions, and (debilitated) associations. Each of these themes manifest differently from person to person, but I believe each provides important contextual analyses where spiritual formation can begin to occur through solidarity with others who are struggling against oppression. Furthermore, the parenthetical adjectives that precede each of them represent potential dangers for multiracial people if their lives are not approached through integrative spiritualities.

First is the spiritual theme of *ancestors.* When tracing multi-

27. I am building on Panikkar's intuition from *Christianity, Part One: The Christian Tradition*, ed. Milena Carrara Pavan (Maryknoll, NY: Orbis Books, 2015), 308–16, where he says that one of the biggest spiritual challenges for Christianity today is to maintain a "mystique of redemption" that is open to both being sustained by (and offered unto) the divine amidst the world's events rather than be drowned in cynicism or despair.

raciality throughout history, one will quickly find how it is fraught with violence from legacies of colonization and institutional racism. For many, this results in a sense of disconnect from one's ancestry. Furthermore, because interracial relationships have only recently become more widely accepted and multiracial people have even more recently been allowed to self-identify in governmental settings, multiracial people do not have the privilege of looking to their past to find many connections that can help them navigate their unique challenges within a racialized society. In this dynamic, it is common for mixed-race people to have questions of rootedness,[28] such as "Who am I?" "Where is home?" and "Where do I belong?" While these questions could be read as universal to humanity, they require a certain sensitivity in light of multi/racial experience(s). Because multiracial people cannot look to ancestry, culture, and tradition through any one lens, a sense of disorientation is often the starting place in their formation. Multiracial populations experience significant challenges of rootlessness, which are further compounded by increasing pressures of forced migration, war, economic devastation, and planetary crisis. Therefore, mixed-race people have some of the most complicated and complex lived experiences, creating fertile ground for outlooks on life that are multifaceted and embracing of rich diversity.

Contemporary trauma and spirituality studies have demonstrated how one's ancestry, generational familial patterns, and cultural histories have significant impacts on one's spiritual well-being.[29] New spiritualities such as the "Ancestral Healing Network" are specifically aimed at assisting people who feel a sense of disconnect from their ancestry and culture(s) and help

28. Pearl Gaskins, *What Are You? Voices of Mixed-Race Young People* (New York: Henry Holt, 1999).

29. Thomas Hübl, *Healing Collective Trauma: A Process for Integrating Our Intergenerational & Cultural Wounds* (Boulder, CO: Sounds True, 2020).

them to integrate the stories of those who have gone before them even if they identified with different cultural or religious traditions.[30] Other spiritual movements are emerging that speak to the heart of those who feel a sense of disconnect from their own multiplicity and encourage a pluralistic approach to spirituality such as the "spiritual but not religious," "new monastics," and the multireligious movements. It is clear that mixed-race people can also contribute significantly to the ongoing emergence of these "new" spiritualities as their lived experiences are already pluralistic in nature.

Second, critical mixed-race studies stress the importance of attitudes when it comes to expressing racialized experiences. Due to the monoracial bias that is still normative and widespread in contemporary anti-racist work in many organizational settings, many multiracial people naturally lean toward attitudes that are fragmented. While mixed-race people disrupt monolithic categories, their both/and mentality gets rejected due to monoracism. As a result, multiracial people experience repeated stigmatization and delegitimization that foster distorted attitudes and internalized oppression. Jessica Harris[31] discusses how multiracial people perpetually devalue and minimize their own racialized experience as a self-protection mechanism that further creates an ongoing absence of mixed-race participation in collective life.

CMRS advocates that *monoracial-* or fixed-identity paradigms negatively affect mental health, and so multiracial people should respond by leading the way in new contextual and agential approaches to racial justice efforts. CMRS proposes

30. Daniel Foor, *Ancestral Medicine: Rituals for Personal and Family Healing* (Rochester, VT: Bear & Company, 2017).

31. See Jessica C. Harris, "Multiracial College Students' Experiences with Multiracial Microaggressions," *Race Ethnicity and Education* 20, no. 4 (July 4, 2017): 429–45.

new and transformed approaches when leading and facilitating anti-racist work that emphasizes polyvocality, power analysis, and the centrality of lived experiences. In current climates of compounded mental health crises, societal polarization, low self-esteem, and fatigue, these emphases only increase in their importance as individuals and communities strive to resist monoracial- or fixed-identity paradigms and avoid re-inscribing essentialized identities.

As spirituality has long been concerned with how to cultivate nonjudgmental attitudes in the interiority of a person to overcome binary or dualistic thinking, the ability to see and affirm multiple perspectives is something that many multiracial people naturally do because of their status as being "both." Spiritualities such as Internal Family Systems (IFS) normalize multiplicity and the acceptance of pluralism, which strongly relates to multi/racial experience(s) and the need to relate to multiracial people's experiences in nonpathologizing and compassionate ways.[32] When considering the nonhierarchical nature of contemplative spirituality, a commitment to plurality can be a vast resource to mixed-race people (and all who are devoted to anti-racism) to help them recognize the dangers of attachment or fixation on any one identity or experience at the expense of others.

Third, multiraciality demonstrates the importance of actions as essential to thriving. For multi/racial experience(s), adaptive action is normative as many are regularly forced to negotiate the nuances and complexities of racialization in ways that monoracial people do not. Through their experiences, multiracial populations offer profound insights to the insidious ways that race and racism persist through monoraciality. However, not all mul-

32. Richard Schwartz, *No Bad Parts: Healing Trauma and Restoring Wholeness with the Internal Family Systems Model* (Louisville, CO: Sounds True, 2021).

tiracial people offer such benefits, as there are many who, when placed in monoracist environments, drown in fear and cling to certainty through devitalized actions such as avoiding, denying, or rejecting their racialized experience. CMRS identifies the need for mixed-race people to improve their capacities to identify liminal moments when they can creatively and adaptively respond to situations and corresponding dynamics of oppression in ways that promote transformation.

Liminality is a profoundly spiritual recognition. Spiritual teacher, mystic, and theologian Barbara Holmes writes about liminality as the space where the impossible becomes possible.[33] Buddhist spiritual insights regarding impermanence bear striking resemblance to the necessity for multiracial people to act with awareness of their contextual "now." In contemplating multiraciality through spirituality, we realize the need for new and previously unimagined possibilities that can disrupt, surprise, and transform racialized encounters. Spirituality encourages embracing liminality through trust, confidence, and courage to act in the face of the unknown that is the future. In resonance with CMRS, racial justice efforts must find ways to acknowledge and embrace liminality. To embrace liminality is risky, but it is needed, if also dangerous, for social change.

Lastly, the spiritual theme of *associations* is clear in multi/racial experience(s). In this historical moment, with people experiencing isolation, mental health challenges, and broad skepticism toward institutional authorities, multiracial people feel the impacts of all these common realities as they are magnified by racial exclusion. The lack of communities to share their unique racialized experiences leaves multiracial people

33. See Barbara Holmes's book *Crisis Contemplation* (Albuquerque, NM: Center of Action and Contemplation, 2021).

and broader collective efforts for racial justice stunted and fragmented.[34] Due to forces of monoracism, mixed-race people are excluded from groups that practice their commitments to racial justice with monoracial bias and thus weaken the bonds of interracial solidarity. While many community organizers and activists now better understand that resistance to oppression is most impactful when it is intersectional and multidimensional, specific awareness of multiraciality is remarkably difficult to find. Even in efforts of race-based activism and resistance, multiracial people still struggle to share their lives openly and honestly for fear that they will be further rejected and minoritized. In order for multiracial organizing to be advanced, there must be an increased emphasis on multiraciality.[35] For those multiracial people who are thriving, one of the key reasons for their thriving is that they have found others who embrace their multiraciality and in so doing offer belonging.

A sense of belonging is of prime importance for spirituality. In fact, the study of spirituality itself is seen by some as an investigation of one's relatedness to all of life. Barbara Holmes writes that spirituality is an "exploration of relatedness as the organizing principle of the universe."[36] Holmes's understanding of spirituality is in line with the key contribution that multiracial people can offer as they relate to many kinds of people and groups based on their own pluralistic experiences. Multi/racial experience(s) are important because they encourage the nurturance of belonging in others as well. Hence, a mixed-race

34. Harris, "Toward a Critical Multiracial Theory in Education."

35. Brooke Barnett and Peter Felten, eds., *Intersectionality in Action: A Guide for Faculty and Campus Leaders for Creating Inclusive Classrooms and Institutions*, 1st ed. (Sterling, VA: Stylus Publishing, 2016).

36. Barbara Holmes and Donny Bryant, "The Cosmic We with Barbara Holmes and Donny Bryant," podcast (2021), https://cac.org/podcast/the cosmic-we.

focus is not only powerful for mixed-race identity-formation efforts but also will fuel anti-racist efforts in partnership with other communities, including but not ending with human communities.

Conclusion

This chapter has laid the foundation for how I understand multi/racial experience(s) through both interdisciplinary (CMRS) and spiritual lenses. This chapter is clear that multiraciality is a social construction and fluid in nature, consistently embracing the experience of "the borderlands" as foundational to one's self-understanding and actions for social justice. While multi/racial experience(s) are diverse, continuously shifting, and cannot be viewed as a static monolith, I also make the claim that multi/racial experience(s) have significant spiritual dimensions to them that can be understood as gifts they offer the larger collective as well as unfulfilled longings and needs. This chapter, then, calls for *spiritual attentiveness* to the lives of mixed-race people. While critical mixed-race studies offer important insights to the ways that racism functions predominantly as monoracism and to the necessity of embracing intercultural and polyperspectival approaches in efforts of liberation, bringing in a spiritual approach can uniquely contribute to the challenges of racism in North America. Although there continues to be persistent marginalization of multi/racial experience(s), there are only growing opportunities for spiritualities to reflect the wisdoms inherent in multi/racial experience(s), supporting and encouraging solidarity with others who are experiencing different kinds of oppressions, re-uniting the interrelationship of contemplation and action.

2

Remembering Raimon Panikkar as a Mixed-Race Prophet

For almost the entirety of my ministry and leadership vocation, I have often started my introduction to others by disclosing my mixed-race social location. Because I am often called upon to publicly communicate and speak to audiences that are racially and ethnically diverse, I would begin by saying: "My name is Aizaiah and I am both Chinese and Mexican. You can call me a Chexican!" In many spaces, people would laugh and warm up to me as a communicator. Obviously (even without me consciously knowing it), one of the ways to view the world that I have internalized is through my otherized and racialized multiplicity. It has always been obvious to me that I am different and that race matters—because of my mixed racial identity I had to be ready for the many ways I would be perceived as *different.* Rather than allowing racialized experiences to prevent connection, I chose to use them to show others the ridiculousness of monolithic thinking. At other times, though, this approach was not advantageous, especially when it was used to appease white normativity and reinforce the permanence of race (in the worst moments this produced a lot of self-deprecation that was not healthy). However, what this does tell me is that race impacts us all more deeply than we know and perhaps there is a way of naming it and bringing illumination to the absurd ways it lays hold of us.

I also have realized since then that understanding my own life and my spirituality cannot happen apart from reflection on the racialization I have experienced. I have come to learn about prayer, worship, justice, and the presence of the sacred in and through my mixedness. It would be not too much to say that I could not understand God without my mixed experience! And as important as it is, I also know that I am more than my racial identification. I live at the intersections of racialized worlds, and yet, at the same time I know I am more through my very being. I cannot reduce myself to any one dimension, yet without any one of them, I would cease to be who I am. My experience is *advaitic* and so is my being. I have come to this interior wisdom through mysticism and spiritual practices that have invited me to know my full self as interconnected to the divine life. I am not separate. No one and nothing are. All is woven together in an interdependent and mysteriously connected reality. It is from this revelation that I attempt to write theology and offer spiritual practices that help others arrive at the place where unity and plurality are interconnected.—*Aizaiah Yong,* journal entry, Los Angeles, CA, 2019

This chapter is dedicated to remembering the life and legacy of Raimon Panikkar as a mixed-race practitioner of religion and spirituality who prophetically offered his own experience to others as a gift so they might deepen theirs. This chapter builds on the four spiritual themes of multi/racial experience(s) that I identified in the previous chapter and specifically focuses on Raimon Panikkar as a person who lived deeply in touch with the spiritual dimensions of multiraciality. This chapter seeks to bear witness to Panikkar's legacy through his own invitation to zoe-ography,[1] proposing how his peculiar biographical elements are responsive to the needs and experience(s) of multiraciality.

First, I begin by locating Panikkar's transformation through his connection to *ancestors* and the ancient roots of monasticism. Second, I discuss Panikkar's contemplative mood as the primary *attitude* that governed his outlook in the world. Third, I focus on two of his most important *actions*: intrareligious dialogue and his pilgrimage to Kailash. Fourth, I reflect on the nurturing *associations* of Panikkar's life as Cosmotheandric—human in his intra- and interpersonal relationships, cosmic through his participation in ecosophy, and divine in touch with the mysticism of Jesus Christ. This chapter concludes with my understanding of the spiritual themes of multiraciality as they were harmonized in Panikkar's own life and in his revolutionary *Cosmotheandric Vision*. The relationship of the four spiritual themes and Panikkar's *Cosmotheandrism* emerges from my analysis of his own experiences as a mixed-race person and remains vitally important for the spiritual formation

1. Panikkar distinguished between the *bios* of his life from the *zoe*. A potentially interesting study would be to look at his "zoe-ography," which was the sacred aspect he knew to be at the core of his being. This is discussed further in *The Water of the Drop: Fragments from Panikkar's Diaries*, ed. Milena Carrara Pavan (Delhi: Indian Society for Promoting Christian Knowledge, 2018), 250.

and well-being of mixed-race people at the intersections of Life in all its plentitude today.

This chapter also stresses how I view Panikkar's mysticism as a major resource that can guide and affirm the rich diversity of multi/racial experience(s) and spiritualities. I am convinced that mixed-race people can know our own lives beyond racialization, while not dismissing or denying its traumatic impacts. I conclude this chapter by sharing the foundations for a spiritual formation program I created called Mysticism, Compassion, and Multiraciality (MCAM), which seeks to engage mixed-race people through practices of mysticism and spirituality so that multiracial populations can find support and new bonds of connection with Life itself.

Blessed Simplicity: Panikkar's Roots in the Archetype of the Monk

One of the driving forces that animated Panikkar's life was to find himself "free from all sense of otherness, his heart filled with the unique experience of the Self: fully, and forever, awake."[2] Noticing the trends of fragmentation that existed around the globe, he often felt out of place wherever he went and longed to discover that which could support him in realizing his truest identity. The answer for him was twofold: "to return to our roots and traditions [listening] to the message left by our mystical tradition . . . taking up the path marked out by our ancestors" and to "strive for cross-fertilization of the various human traditions."[3] Panikkar discovered one such "way"

2. These are a few lines Panikkar lifted from a text that was reproduced by Swami Abhishiktananda from the *Brhadaranyaka,* found in Raimon Panikkar, *Mysticism and Spirituality, Part Two: Spirituality, the Way of Life*, ed. Milena Carrara Pavan (Maryknoll, NY: Orbis Books. 2014), 150.

3. Panikkar, *Mysticism and Spirituality, Part Two,* xvi.

to these ends, that which he referred to as "the archetype of the monk."[4] In his words, "the monk is the expression of an archetype that is a constitutive dimension of human life . . . and there is a primordial monastic dimension prior to the qualification of being Christian, Buddhist, and the like . . . this distinction is transcendental."[5] For Panikkar, the monastic archetype[6] allows for both rootedness in tradition and the power to participate in what he called *incarnatio continua*.[7] The monastic "archetype is a unique quality of each person, which at once needs and shuns institutionalization" and is also a "highly personal adventure."[8] He expressed his monastic vocation as a life in solidarity with humanity that must "assimilate the wisdom of bygone traditions and, having made it our own . . . allow it to grow. Life," he wrote, "is neither repetition nor continuation. It is growth, which implies at once rupture and continuity. Life is creation."[9]

Rather than affiliation with any one particular group, Panikkar described the monastic way as living in touch with the "human invariant," that aspect of life which can be experienced within diverse cultural and religious traditions across the world and allows for Life to be carried on and renewed.[10] He spoke of his own journey as both a continuation of ancient tradition that

4. Panikkar, *Mysticism and Spirituality, Part Two,* 133.

5. Panikkar, *Mysticism and Spirituality, Part Two,* 138.

6. Raimon Panikkar, *The Rhythm of Being: The Unbroken Trinity* (Maryknoll, NY: Orbis Books, 2010), xxvi.

7. For Panikkar, *incarnatio continua* was the process by which Life embraces itself as it continually transforms. In Panikkarian thought, creation is not a one-time event but something at the core of reality altogether. See *The Water of the Drop,* 281.

8. Panikkar, *Mysticism and Spirituality, Part Two,* 134.

9. Panikkar, *The Rhythm of Being,* xxvii.

10. One will find numerous references in Panikkar's journal to how he resisted identifying totally with any one group, but rather the "life of the 'I' that transcends the ego." One such example can be found in his entry of October 6, 1969. See *The Water of the Drop,* 478.

invites polarities to harmonize through creative tension and a creation of his own unique personal path. The archetype of the monk, he wrote,

> is something special, difficult, even sometimes queer, with tinges of social and cultural nonconformity; on the other hand, it is something so very much human that it is ultimately claimed to be the vocation of every human being, what everybody should be or is called upon to be—in some way or other, sooner or later. An enlightened awareness of this polarity will, I hope, put us on the right track in our quest.[11]

When looking back on the uniqueness of Panikkar's monastic life, it is also clear he did not want to isolate himself from the world. Panikkar wrote, "Since my early youth, I have seen myself as a monk but one without a monastery, or at least without walls other than those of the entire planet."[12] Consequentially, Panikkar's life and actions were guided by and indebted to the conscious embrace of ancestral roots and through his embrace of it, his experience deepened.[13] Through the embrace of ancestral connections, multiracial populations are invited to a reclamation of all the wisdom that dominant cultures have attempted to deny, erase, and forget.

11. Panikkar, *Mysticism and Spirituality, Part Two,* 132.

12. Panikkar, *Mysticism and Spirituality, Part Two,* 130.

13. One example of how the ancestral roots of the monastic archetype influenced Panikkar is through the nine rules, or sutra, he gave himself. Panikkar's personal nine sutra can be found as his response to a question about what kind of meditation should be pursued. He responded in Panikkaresque fashion, saying, "I do not have a method, a technique I could recommend. I believe that all techniques are useful and that all of them are obstacles as well," as he found both roots to grow from (and be disciplined by) and a cosmic confidence for the transformation of the world. See *A Dwelling Place for Wisdom* (Louisville, KY: Westminster-John Knox Press, 1993), 156.

A Life Fully Lived: Panikkar's Contemplative Mood

In the foreword to his distinguished *Opera Omnia* collection, Panikkar observes that all the writings in the collection "are not the fruit of mere speculation but rather are autobiographical, i.e., firstly they were inspired by a life and praxis which were only molded into writing later on."[14] Here, Panikkar expressed a profound self-understanding that was foundational to all his intellectual offerings to the world. Namely, that Life was to be lived and not only theorized about. I argue that this brief remark reveals Raimon Panikkar's primary gift to humanity, namely, that Life is to be embodied, experienced, and co-created. Rather than limit the scope of his prolific writings to esoteric concepts and/or interesting neologisms, the volumes in the collection represent Panikkar's devout commitment to live his life as a contemplative practice.

In terms of the disparate disciplines of modern academic theology, Panikkar was not a practical theologian in any explicit sense. Yet his intense convictions that theological and philosophical writing ought to deepen and transform Life clearly situate him as a thinker and prophet whom practical theology should take seriously. "Writing, to me, is meditation—that is medicine—and moderation, order for this world. Writing, to me, is intellectual life and that in turn is spiritual existence," he observed. Particularly for practical theologians who attend to the intricate relationships of a pluralist world, Panikkar's own thoughts about writing reveal a spiritual leader who was deeply concerned for the holistic and lived integration of spirituality. He continued, "The climax of life is, in my opinion, to

14. Series foreword, *Opera Omnia* (Maryknoll, NY: Orbis Books, 2014–22).

participate in the life of the universe, in both the cosmic and divine symphonies to which even we mortals are invited. It is not only a matter of living but also of letting life be—this life, offered to us as a gift so that we may sustain and deepen it."[15] Furthermore, Panikkar's attitude toward his own engagement with the world was shaped by his vocation as a priest.[16] Paying attention to the ways that liberation related him to others, he wrote, "I may try to liberate myself or more precisely, to contribute to the work of my liberation. I may try to help my neighbour do the same."[17] With his insistence that theology must be in touch with concrete life experience in relational ways that are transformational,[18] Panikkar emerges as an amenable dialogue partner for contemporary practical theology.

Although Panikkar repeatedly emphasized the importance of concrete living (orthopraxy), he also shared publicly his reluctance to historicize his legacy, wanting instead to keep focus on his life as but one expression of the *fullness of Life* itself.[19] For this

15. Panikkar, *A Dwelling Place for Wisdom*, 79.

16. Panikkar saw himself in the prophetic priesthood lineage beginning a "new line" and "referring back to Melchizedek, who had no forefathers." See *The Water of the Drop*, 97.

17. Panikkar, *The Water of the Drop*, 328.

18. Panikkar's primordial commitment to the actuality of life is incarnated through his awareness of "tempiternity," as well as his revolutionary interreligious spiritual practice, "intrareligious dialogue," inviting practitioners from across religious and cultural traditions to relate to one another out of reverence, humility, conviction, and gratitude. See "Glossary: Tempiternity" and "Glossary: Dialogical Dialogue," Fundació Vivarium Raimon Panikkar, 2022.

19. Panikkar wrote in the foreword to his *Opera Omnia:* "The decision to publish this collection of my writings has not been easy and, more than once, I have had to overcome the 'temptation' to abandon the attempt, the reason being that, though I fully subscribe to the Latin saying that *scripta manent* [texts remain], I also firmly believe that what actually matters in the final analysis is to live out Life; this has been demonstrated by the great masters who, as Thomas Aquinas affirms citing Pythagoras and Socrates in the

reason, I argue that the best way to honor the life and thought of Panikkar is to commit one's own life to the same vision that he realized in his being, or perhaps to the same *mood* by which he lived. Panikkar spoke of "the contemplative mood"[20] as that which "is connected with the very purpose of life and not a means to anything else."[21] I contend that the contemplative mood runs throughout his works, including the *Opera Omnia* and *The Water of the Drop: Fragments from Panikkar's Diaries.* Furthermore, the contemplative mood is a hermeneutical challenge to practical theologies that seek to spiritually undergird anti-racist efforts in our world today. Panikkar's personal diary reveals his life path as simultaneously affirming differences yet avoiding attachment to any one label or identification, knowing that all perspectives have their limits. "Am I trying to become a (better) Christian? (Or a better Hindu?)," he asked. "I don't like labels. But I think so. To me it means that I am trying to finish the process of Incarnation (the fusion—without confusion—of the Divine and the Human) in me. It means to become Christ. So," he concluded, "it means I am trying to become fully Man and at the same time fully God. It might be better to say fully Human and fully Divine."[22] As he lived out his calling, he was strengthened by the examples of contemplatives who had gone

Summa (but not Buddha, whom he could not know of), did not actually write a single word." See *Opera Omnia*, series foreword.

20. Raimon Panikkar, *Mysticism and Spirituality, Part One: Mysticism, the Fullness of Life*, ed. Milena Carrara Pavan (Maryknoll, NY: Orbis Books, 2014), 31.

21. Panikkar expounds on how the "contemplative spirit" is resistant to the major supremacies plaguing collective life in contemporary time including but not limited to Christian/religious supremacy, secular supremacy, economic supremacy, scientific/technological supremacy, and victor/war-based supremacy. See *Mysticism and Spirituality, Part One*, 31–42.

22. Panikkar, *The Water of the Drop*, 152.

before him, learning from their insights and incorporating them into his own life.

Mary and the Feminine Dimension

From early in his life, Mary, the Virgin Mother of God, played a significant role in Panikkar's spiritual life and contemplative mood. In the second entry of *The Water of the Drop*, Panikkar references his high esteem for "the Blessed Virgin" when he was twelve years old.

> Most Holy Mary, Virgin Mother of God, I, Raimundo Panikkar, although most unworthy of being thy servant. Yet moved by thy wonderful mercy and by the desire to serve thee, choose thee today in the presence of my guardian angel and the whole heavenly court, for my special lady, Advocate and Mother; and I firmly resolve that I will serve thee always and do whatever I can to induce others to serve thee.[23]

Later in his life, Panikkar included text from a retreat he gave that focused on Mary in an introduction to *Opera Omnia*.

> This text is a simple confession of my love for Mary, Mother of God, symbol of humanity in which the divine is fully manifested—not in an abstract humanity, but in each person who knows how to utter Mary's unreserved yes.[24]

Mary's *yes* inspired Panikkar to claim that a recovery of the *feminine* dimension of life is what was needed most for spiritu-

23. Panikkar, *The Water of the Drop*, 4.
24. Panikkar, *Mysticism and Spirituality, Part Two*, 66.

alities today. He wrote, "Mary is the living symbol of a human religion, and of a religion that has a human aspect: we are the female principle that God fertilizes."[25] "Feminine" here does not so much refer to a specific gender identity but instead stems from a stance that is open and receptive to the mysterious unfolding of Life. This receptive posture is vital for those seeking liberation from oppression as they face the various and challenging ways that they are interiorly cut off from their innate power, dignity, and value.[26] Oppressed people need new paths that can allow previously unnoticed resources to emerge. For Panikkar, Mary is one such figure who demonstrates a recovery of an open and receptive attitude toward life even amid marginalization as well as a posture of faith, integrating multiple experiences (especially those that are marginalized) through wisdom and love.

The Examples of Clare, Francis of Assisi, John of the Cross, and Teresa of Avila

Other contemplatives who greatly influenced Panikkar were those "spiritual pairs of male and female who worked together and mutually enhanced each other's spiritual life."[27] He highlighted Clare with Francis of Assisi and John of the Cross with Teresa of Avila in his volume on mysticism as "examples of holi-

25. Panikkar, *Mysticism and Spirituality, Part Two,* 115.

26. Panikkar's book *Cultural Disarmament* (Minneapolis: Fortress Press, 1995) was a political work aimed at calling for colonial ways of being and relating to be decentered and surrendered as the necessary prerequisite for peace to be received. In this book, Panikkar heavily emphasized the role of listening to those who have been marginalized. Panikkar believed that listening could only be fostered by reclaiming the feminine dimensions at the core of one's being.

27. Michiko Yusa, "Intercultural Philosophical Wayfaring: An Autobiographical Account in Conversation with a Friend," *Journal of World Philosophies* 3, no. 1 (May 31, 2018): 123–34.

ness," who mastered the "art of living" in and through embrace of "bare" human experience in authenticity.[28] Panikkar recalls three movements that Clare practiced, allowing her to flow with the divine as *intuere* (aim), *considera* (consider), and *contempla* (contemplate). Panikkar described these three movements as achieving harmony with the "first, second, and third eye," transforming the world by "not withdrawing into another life . . . but transforming ourselves and the part of reality entrusted to us."[29] It was the simplicity of Clare's spirituality that Panikkar loved most as she did not seek extravagant living but to touch the depth of each moment with infinite love.

Similarly, Panikkar perceived divine love embodied in the simplicity of everyday life through the witnesses of Teresa of Avila and John of the Cross. "Despite the rich spiritualities and high mystical gifts with which they were endowed," he wrote, "they do not exclusively push or preach contemplation, mysticism, and the like; they do not want anyone to deny the world, nor do they make self-denial their central doctrine. They simply preach and live a holy life—that is to say, holiness, pure and simple. . . ."[30] From these two contemplatives, Panikkar received a raw and naked spiritual simplicity that deepened his own attitude toward his vocation in the lineage of the *monachos*, the lineage of the "person who aspires to reach the ultimate goal of life with all his being by renouncing all that is not necessary to it—that is by concentrating on this one single and unique goal."[31] All of these contemplative examples served as the guides who encouraged Panikkar to embrace a contemplative approach in all he did. And through new attitudes of self-compassion,

28. Panikkar, *Mysticism and Spirituality, Part One,* 93.
29. Panikkar, *Mysticism and Spirituality, Part One,* 96–97.
30. Panikkar, *Mysticism and Spirituality, Part One,* 104.
31. Panikkar, *Mysticism and Spirituality, Part Two,* 133.

curiosity, and contemplation, multiracial populations can be supported with inner resources to weather the onslaught of monoracism and structural patterns of racialization.

Intrareligious Dialogue and a Pilgrimage to Kailash: Panikkar's Unique Spiritual Practices

In addition to approaching life as contemplative practice, Panikkar also created and led others in novel spiritual practices that enriched their lives. Joseph Prabhu described the world-renowned Easter celebrations that Panikkar would often facilitate in Santa Barbara, California.[32] Through his unique approach to liturgy, Panikkar led visitors from across the world in deepening their awareness of and intimate connectedness with the plenitude of Life itself, honoring the elements of the cosmos, the cultural insights from around the world, and a reverence for the mysterious presence of the sacred.[33] In his public practice, Panikkar demonstrated his conviction that spirituality and spiritual practices were not to be reserved for private benefit as if the individual person was disconnected from the rest of the cosmos. Though he certainly engaged many practices from across monastic spiritualities, there are two important spiritual practices he uniquely created that I would like to highlight: intrareligious dialogue and pilgrimage to Kailash.

32. One example of how Panikkar-led cosmotheandric liturgical services would unfold can be found in his journal entry from April 11, 1971. See *The Water of the Drop*, 71.

33. Joseph Prabhu, "Roots, Routes, and a New Awakening: Walking and Meditating with Raimon Panikkar," in Ananta Kumar Giri, ed., *Roots, Routes and a New Awakening: Beyond One and Many and Alternative Planetary Futures* (Singapore: Palgrave Macmillan, 2021).

Intrareligious Dialogue

Raimon Panikkar famously described his interreligious life: "I left Europe [for India] as a Christian, discovered I was Hindu, returned a Buddhist, without ever having ceased to be a Christian."[34] His experiences of religious multiplicity came from his own pluralistic ethnic heritage but also emerged through the intimate relationships he fostered with diverse cultural and religious communities. Panikkar was adamant not to speculate about religions from a distance but to experience them from within. His approach to this was what he referred to as the "intrareligious dialogue," which he identified as "a path to survival."[35] Intrareligious dialogue was his own way of opening himself interiorly to differences. Panikkar thought comparative theology or philosophy must be engaged both logically/discursively and through the depth dimension of the heart and spirit. Panikkar was convinced that there was a difference between knowing *about* religion and knowing *of* religion through religious experience. In his intrareligious dialogue practice, Panikkar worked to overcome modernity's temptation to rationalize everything as a problem to be solved. He insisted on an intimate relationship with the infinite uniqueness of each person, culture, and tradition through love. Teaching intrareligious dialogue to others, Panikkar would often use the metaphor of a *window*:

> We all see through windows. We see better, the cleaner our window is. I need you to tell me that I am looking through a window. Nobody alone can find anything—we need each other. And today in the present politi-

34. "Laudatio," Fundació Vivarium Raimon Panikkar, 2022.

35. Raimon Panikkar, *Cultures and Religions in Dialogue, Part Two: Intercultural and Interreligious Dialogue*, ed. Milena Carrara Pavan (Maryknoll, NY: Orbis Books, 2018), xiii.

> cal, economic, and world situation, no single person, no single system, no single religion, can deal with the human condition or can claim to offer the solution of the problems of our planet. It is either solidarity on all levels or we go to catastrophe. We realize our neighbor helps us and here begins the intrareligious dialogue. You say your narrative. You say what you see. You say what you hear. You say what you believe. You share your experience. And be ready at the same time to hear the other telling other narratives, other beliefs, other experiences. And then we dialogue.[36]

Panikkar demonstrates through the metaphor of the window how one should engage racial, religious, ethnic, and cultural differences from deep interiority, spaciousness, and conversation with one another. He remained careful to distinguish this type of dialogue as "dialogical," one that is relational, spiritual, and involving one's holistic being. In dialogical dialogue, Panikkar invites the individual to realize human dignity as an awakening to "contingency . . . [to not possessing] total all-round vision." For, truly, "nobody does" because "reality itself [is] pluralistic," and humans "are not only spectators of Reality, but also cofactors and even coauthors of it."[37] Intrareligious dialogue really was a core element of all Panikkar's writings and his life practice, as he consistently gave himself to a path of inquiry and integration. And it was through his conviction of intrareligious dialogue that Panikkar was then led to his "ultimate" spiritual practice, a pilgrimage to Kailash.

36. Stillpoint: The Center for Christian Spirituality, "Raimon Panikkar: The Window," video (September 5, 2015); www.youtube.com.

37. Raimon Panikkar, *Cultures and Religions in Dialogue, Part One: Pluralism and Interculturality*, ed. Milena Carrara Pavan (Maryknoll, NY: Orbis Books, 2018), xvii.

Pilgrimage to Kailash

Raimon Panikkar often referred to his life as "pilgrimage."[38] In an authentic sense, Panikkar understood himself to be a sojourner, a co-participant with all beings in Cosmotheandric solidarity. In fact, he dedicated his pilgrimage to assist other seekers, as he wrote, "[those who] perhaps wish to be supported by the experience of other pilgrims."[39] At the tender age of 76, Raimon Panikkar risked his life, embarking on a pilgrimage to Kailash,[40] a "practice" not "theory (orthodoxy) but action (orthopraxy)."[41] Panikkar wrote that his purpose was to "go up there only to be there for no other purpose" and "to give up all commitments and activities that are important to him, uncertain even that he will be able to resume them on his return."[42] After his pilgrimage experience, Panikkar described a threefold transformation "taking place in the microcosm of self, also having repercussions in the macrocosm." He understood his practice as one of Cosmotheandric reconciliation, "making peace" with humanity (overcoming all exclusivism),[43] the cosmos (overcoming alienation and estrangement from the land), and the

38. One such example is from his journal entry on February 21, 1980. See *The Water of the Drop,* 120.

39. Raimon Panikkar and Milena Carrara Pavan, *A Pilgrimage to Kailash* (New Delhi: Motilal Banarsidass, 2018), 152.

40. Mount Kailash is considered to be a sacred site for multiple religious traditions including Tibetan Buddhism and Hinduism, so Panikkar naturally chose this site for its interreligious histories and foundations. It was also a place Panikkar's father always wanted to go, and, by embarking on this journey, he fulfilled a karmic desire. As Kailash is known as one of the most dangerous pilgrimages due to the fact that its paths are not clearly marked, the weather is extreme, the altitudes are intense, and there are no hotels or inns to rest at, Panikkar knew if he was to return it would be sheer grace. See *A Pilgrimage to Kailash,* 15.

41. Panikkar and Pavan, *A Pilgrimage to Kailash,* 15.

42. Panikkar and Pavan, *A Pilgrimage to Kailash,* 17.

43. In his journal, Panikkar described the pilgrimage as consciously

gods (making sacrifice to appease the wrath and discord of the gods).[44] Panikkar's pilgrimage was no small feat, as he wrote, "To go to Kailasa, is the definitive and final pilgrimage, the supreme one. . . . Like any ultimate experience, this pilgrimage is ineffable. . . . Ultimate means it is a pilgrimage of no return. If by chance you do return, it is by pure grace: you have become a new being."[45]

He felt as though he did return as a new being, later writing that the pilgrimage was "a turning point" in his life that could be marked by "the physical change in [his] heart [that] became the outward sign" of his transformation. He described pilgrimage experiences of an emerging awareness of his profound solidarity with other creatures "when [he] could not breathe during the interminable nights." He described the interconnectivity that undergirded his experiences, writing, "I was aware that our fellow beings are also suffocating the Earth. Man is a microcosm because the Earth is also a *macranthropos*. We are all interconnected. . . . My pilgrimage was . . . simply sharing both the human and earthly condition."[46] Further, Panikkar's experiences of his own fragile humanity (and perhaps the divinity that pierces through such fragility) deepened through his pilgrimage to Kailash. For Panikkar, recognizing the danger and perils that come with living into the risks and mysteries of Life in each moment became a gift of this ultimate spiritual practice. Pilgrimage to Kailash deepened his reliance in cosmic confidence. That is, pilgrimage vivified his witness of surrender to Life's continuous unfolding in all of its nakedness, fragility, impermanence, and interconnectedness. And these two practices serve

---

"Breaking a double anti-ecumenical Exclusivism." See *The Water of the Drop*, 188.

44. Panikkar and Pavan, *A Pilgrimage to Kailash*, 20.
45. Panikkar and Pavan, *A Pilgrimage to Kailash*, 19.
46. Panikkar, *The Water of the Drop*, 189.

as a powerful reminder for multiracial people that they too can create new kinds of spiritual practices that weave together their own knowings and ways of being.

A Christophanic Example: Relationships That Cultivated Panikkar's Mysticism

While Panikkar's mysticism is unique, he did not come to it in isolation but through intimate relations with Life. Four relationships or *associations* that were vital for his Cosmotheandric Vision (and which I contend are crucial for a practical theology of multiraciality today) were (1) his relationship with his innermost being, (2) interpersonal relationships, (3) his relationship with the cosmos, and (4) relationship with the divine, namely, what he called the "mysticism of Jesus Christ." This section addresses each of these associations and then concludes with a discussion of Christophany, his idiosyncratic form of mysticism that emerged through the culmination of these four associations.

Panikkar had a strong relationship with his own interiority in a few critical ways. His intellectual writings are the first evidence of this strong relationship. However, he was the first to recognize that his immense scholarship was fueled from within, by a burning spiritual desire, because he believed that any meaningful transformation could not be the result of "outside" pressure upon him. For Panikkar, writing was a primary way in which he realized his own experience more profoundly, weaving together his observations, his intellect, and his spiritual intuition. His intellectual writing, however, was not the only writing that formed his own relationship within himself. Beginning as a teen, Panikkar practiced journaling "to perfect [himself] by writing something [he had] done, whether good or bad, during the day and let it be the norm of [his] action."[47] Journaling helped him to unify what would otherwise have been fragments within himself. Recognizing his own multiplicity, he wrote,

> Too many things, too many worlds, cultures, environments, languages, religions, people! Should I hold back, limit myself? Do I perhaps have too many me's? Can I manage them all? I am a philosopher . . . I am a theologian . . . I am a priest. . . . What image of myself should I project? Today is Tuesday, my day of reflection. It is good to spend a day in complete silence, absorbed in prayer and meditation without restriction of time.[48]

Along with the recognition of his own diverse presences to himself, journaling gave Panikkar opportunities for regular self-evaluation. "The truth," he wrote, "is I am always questioning myself and trying to be open to change, to metanoia—and not having anybody with whom I could talk these matters over, I have to resort to my diary."[49] These brief excerpts represent his own awareness of the diverse aspects present within himself as well as the critical role that journaling played in cultivating his own spiritual life, renewing him with capacities to travail the depths of his life through compassion.

Second, Panikkar was supported in his own formation through congenial relationships with others who were attempting to harmonize wisdom by cross-fertilizing cultural and religious traditions from the East and West, with deep commitments to mysticism and spirituality. Two are particularly important here: Swami Abhishiktananda, also known as Henri Le Saux (1910–1973), and his disciple, Milena Carrara Pavan.

47. Panikkar, *The Water of the Drop*, 3.
48. Panikkar, *The Water of the Drop*, 46.
49. Panikkar, *The Water of the Drop*, 100.

Henri Le Saux was a well-known French Benedictine monk who moved to India as a missionary and yet found himself as the one transformed. In his journal, Panikkar described his relationship with Henri Le Saux, writing, "His [Le Saux's] words reverberate in me, they produce the anamnesis of same experiences. It seems as if I were there also. And certainly, I have gone through a very similar[50] odyssey."[51] The same experiences Panikkar references in his writing emerged through the mystical connection that the two shared.

As I emphasized the approaches to plurality and multiplicity in Critical Mixed-Race Studies in the previous chapter, I argue that the shared mystical connection that Panikkar and Abhishiktananda shared should be understood with attention to multiplicity amid prescribed social conventions of monoculturality. For Panikkar, Abhishiktananda was "a friend, a mentor, an example" (2007). In a letter to Le Saux written after Le Saux's death, Panikkar described his personal resonance with Le Saux's life as "a unique path" and "the example" for his own life. Panikkar expressed the rare integration of East and West that Le Saux embodied, writing, "You came to India to make Christ known to Hindus and were converted to the supreme experience of Indic wisdom-advaita."[52] While they only saw each other on occasion, Panikkar's emphasis on the need for radical metanoia and cross-fertilization in his own life and intellectual work was indebted to his association with Henri Le Saux. A practical theology of multiraciality that encourages those of us who seek to experience spiritual healing and well-being for resistance to monoracial supremacy must recognize that the friend-

50. Another example of similarity that Panikkar recognized is found later in his journal when he wrote, "perhaps I am living in a different way than I detected in Abhishiktananda." See *The Water of the Drop,* 95.

51. Panikkar, *The Water of the Drop,* 90.

52. Panikkar, *Cultures and Religions in Dialogue, Part Two,* 273–74.

ship Panikkar describes was profoundly enriched by both men integrating their own multiplicities within themselves and with one another.

Another important relationship for Panikkar was with his disciple, Milena Carrara Pavan, to whom he entrusted his most personal diaries as well as the completion of his life's culminating work, *Opera Omnia*. Through their relationship, Panikkar was invited to be more authentically human and to realize his own Cosmotheandric experience by revealing more fully his "clear side as well as dark side."[53] Quoting Panikkar, Pavan reflected that their relationship was like "the relationship between master and disciple [that] reaches its zenith when the two of them become a mirror for each other" rather than a relationship that sought to hide imperfections. Pavan continues,

> At that point, the relationship is transformed into a true and deep friendship: there is no longer master nor a disciple, just the image they reflect—the image of God—conscious of being that very image, despite its imperfection. The fact of showing myself to you as I am, without disassembling, can also help me to analyze my life, a life that is drawing to a close, and I can help you to learn, also through my mistakes.[54]

Panikkar responded to Pavan's sense of being a mirror with a deeper awareness of himself, writing that, perhaps, she was right. "It would have been useful for me," Panikkar wrote, "to have a guide to help me see the psychological aspect that I neglected, since the spiritual sphere and the intellectual sphere were always predominant in me." In their relationship, Panikkar

53. Panikkar and Pavan, *A Pilgrimage to Kailash*, 152.
54. Panikkar and Pavan, *A Pilgrimage to Kailash*, 152.

was awakened to the implications of an individual's intellectual insights, noting, "I have always claimed that to follow the pure heart is enough, but we need someone to tell us that it is not always so pure. . . . My greatest shortcoming was my presumption, the pride of believing to be highly intellectually gifted and to be endowed with spiritual gifts." While he certainly was so endowed, it was through the mirror of Pavan that Panikkar came to "understand now that I am not fulfilled, that the gifts given to me are not completely embodied in me, transforming my nature. I can now recognize this and admit it serenely."[55] Panikkar and Pavan's relationship supported them both in their transformation as fellow-beings in the banquet of Life together. As Panikkar concluded, "A master is not someone who represents a model for one's life; rather, he is the good friend . . . a channel for the Spirit. In turn, the disciple reflects the Spirit he/she perceives through the master, so that it returns to him renewed. This perichoresis can only take place in a profound relationship of true friendship."[56]

These two important relationships portray the vast significance of close relationships for the well-being of one's life. Intimate friendships can be especially difficult for those who are committed to the spiritual life. When reading through the insights of CMRS, this difficulty can be understood as an even greater challenge for those people who do not fit in to neatly fashioned social groups or identities, such as multiracial people. Panikkar was grateful to find a few with whom he could live into transformation at the borders of East and West. His most profound intellectual contributions are best understood through his relationships of mutuality and shared spiritual aspirations with others. Panikkar's profound interpersonal relationships

55. Panikkar and Pavan, *A Pilgrimage to Kailash*, 155.
56. Panikkar and Pavan, *A Pilgrimage to Kailash*, 157.

bear witness to the theme of associations that promote wholeness, which was identified in an earlier chapter's attention to multi/racial experience(s).

Third, Panikkar had a unique relationship with the cosmos, matter, and Mother Earth that was greatly nurtured by his doctoral studies in chemistry. Reflecting on his time studying the sciences, he said, "I do not regret the seven long years, to get in touch with matter, very intimately!" In his own experience, he reflected on the living and listening communion that he had with the cosmos and pondered this communion in his journal. "Material things have a dynamism, tendency, a conscious structure: physical life. Plants have sensitivity. Animals perceive. Men know that they know," he wrote.[57] Through these and other similar experiences, Panikkar understood nature as a co-constitutive and important aspect of Reality itself, and this became the basis of his proposal for "ecosophy."

Ecosophy is "beyond simple ecology, ecosophy is a wisdom-spirituality of the earth." Ecosophy was the word Panikkar created to clarify the need for new ways of listening that are not anthropocentric. He continued, "The 'new equilibrium' is not so much between man and the earth, as between matter and spirit, between spatio-temporality and consciousness. Ecosophy is neither a mere science of the earth nor wisdom about the earth but rather the wisdom of the earth herself that is made manifest to man when he knows how to listen to her with love."[58] One of Panikkar's most powerful ecosophic moments came from his pilgrimage to Kailash, when he understood the "sermon on the mount to be a sermon of the mount . . . as he listened to the mountain hearing 'these are All blessed'" and ultimately

57. Panikkar, *The Water of the Drop,* 86.

58. "Glossary: Ecosophy," Fundació Vivarium Raimon Panikkar, 2022.

realizing "the sermon on the mount is the sermon: Kailasa."[59] Others have begun to reflect on how ecosophy may be something intuitive to Indigenous traditions.[60] We would do well to center these wisdoms amid growing ecological crisis. Regardless if a turn to ecosophy will happen on a large scale, nurturing his relations with the cosmos was vital[61] for Panikkar's development and remains essential in our longed-for healing. Healing along with the cosmos is especially important for those who suffer from wounds of white supremacist racism because of the ways in which racial oppression has depended on and deepened a deadly transformation of land into property, splitting land from Life, body from mind, and relatives from one another.

Finally, Panikkar was supported by his relationship with the Divine. Milena Carrara Pavan describes Panikkar's "constant reference to God: a daily dialogue with God, firstly an anthropomorphic God, but afterwards an increasingly mysterious presence slowly changing from external to internal, alternating with moments of emptiness."[62] Panikkar was a devoted religious person, a seeker who was always open to the ever-new revelation of the sacred in Life and not confined to particular institutions of religion. He described his own spiritual experience as *Christophanic,* following the lead and mysticism of Jesus Christ of Nazareth. Panikkar discussed Jesus Christ with a sincere reverence and admiration, writing in his journal, "We all need

59. Panikkar and Pavan, *A Pilgrimage to Kailash*, 22.

60. Gerard Hall and Joan Hendriks, *Dreaming a New Earth: Raimon Panikkar and Indigenous Spiritualities* (Ontario: Mosaic Press, 2013); Aseem Shrivastava, "A Time for Ecosophy," *Open Magazine* (blog), openthe magazine.com, May 1, 2020.

61. Panikkar's ecosophic intuition perhaps was also the inspiration for his *Quaternitas Perfecta: The Fourfold Nature of Man,* which spoke to the four centers of Man in conversation with the four elemental symbols of earth, water, fire, and air. See *Cultures and Religions in Dialogue, Part Two,* 329.

62. Panikkar and Pavan, *A Pilgrimage to Kailash*, 152.

one another, and we need a guru. Jesus has been my guru . . . I love you, Lord! You are my first love and the name I learned was Christ!"[63] Panikkar finally understood his relationship with Jesus Christ mystically as "an *Alter*—the other part of [him] self." Panikkar confessed elsewhere, "I have not mentioned you by your name, Jesus Christ. I love you, you who are neither myself nor another."[64] Panikkar knew Jesus Christ as a central and living symbol or *mythos* of transformation in his personal life. From his interpersonal relationship with Christ, Panikkar boldly called other Christians to new ways of practice that would be suitable for the contemporary age of pluralism, a new way of devotion that he called *Christianness.*[65] Panikkar concluded that Jesus Christ offers a vision that is relevant for every human and not reducible to a historical religion. "The mysticism of Jesus Christ is simply human mysticism. What else could it be? It is the ultimate experience of man as Man," Panikkar wrote.[66] For Panikkar, Jesus Christ is about teaching what liberated life feels like. "Jesus," he argued, "achieved a total transparency and transcended both the burden of the past and the fear of the future."[67]

Panikkar referred to one's realization of this mystery as the *Christophanic experience*, an experience that is distinctly Christian yet not reducible to any one religious tradition or institution. Panikkar described the Christophanic experience as a person's life becoming one with Christ, harmonizing polarities in one's innermost being. He wrote, "This is Trinitarian life; this is the Christophanic experience: neither the mere dualism of mere creatureliness, the worldly, nor the monistic simplification

63. Panikkar, *The Water of the Drop*, 92, 135.

64. Panikkar, *The Water of the Drop*, 289.

65. Raimon Panikkar, *Christianity, Part Two: Christophany*, ed. Milena Carrara Pavan (Maryknoll, NY: Orbis Books, 2016), xviii.

66. Panikkar, *Christianity, Part Two*, 238.

67. Panikkar, *Christianity, Part Two,* 230.

of divinization."[68] Through this relational and emergent Christophanic experience, the interrelationality of Life is engaged and transformed.

Christophany is a key concept for understanding Panikkar's Cosmotheandric Vision. For Panikkar, Christophany radicalized his theological work on Trinity and connected with his understanding of *advaita*—that which overcomes all dualisms and monism. In his journal he wrote, "To live my identity, our identity, is a terrific experience. This is *advaita*"[69] Panikkar's *advaitic* outlook was a trans-historical and trans-cultural intuition, weaving together the multiple religious and cultural traditions with which he identified. Through a trans-historical and trans-cultural frame, Panikkar allowed for mystery to be known in ways that transcended historical expressions while being careful to not negate or minimize particularities. Joseph Prabhu described the implications of Panikkar's Christophany, writing, "For those who have the right cosmovision [referring to Christophany], everything is holy and not just the so-called sacred, which is why Panikkar speaks of sacred secularity."[70]

Ultimately, Panikkar's mysticism is a call to overcome "a tribal Christology by a Christophany which allows Christians to see the work of Christ everywhere, without assuming that they have a better grasp or monopoly of that Mystery, which has been revealed to them in a unique way."[71] Weaving a practical theology of multi/racial experience(s) with the mystical and prophetic multiracial example of Raimon Panikkar is crucial for other mixed-race people today. Panikkar's multiraciality played a pivotal role in leading him to these mystical insights, for it

68. Panikkar, *Christianity, Part Two,* 139.
69. Panikkar, *The Water of the Drop*, 273–74.
70. Panikkar, *Cultures and Religions in Dialogue, Part Two,* 36.
71. Panikkar, *Mysticism and Spirituality*, 161.

opened his awareness to and embodiment of multiplicity in religious traditions and cultural communities, allowing him to deepen his own experience of the fullness of Life.

Following Panikkar to (Multiracial) Christophany

(Mixed) Race as Identification and Christophany as Identity

Throughout this chapter, I have argued that considering Raimon Panikkar's life and Christophanic example through the lens of multiraciality reveals how he directly and indirectly lived responsively to the spiritual themes and needs of multiraciality: ancestors, attitudes, actions, and associations. Panikkar wrote that Christophany "constitutes the deepest interiority of all of us, the abyss in which, in each one of us, there is a meeting between the finite and the infinite, the material and the spiritual, the cosmic and the divine."[72]

Panikkar's call to Christophany "emphasizes the difference between *identification* and *identity* which, though inseparable, are not the same thing. The former is *what* an individual is, including all the physical information . . . the latter is *who* a person is in his or her deepest reality."[73] By following Panikkar's Christophanic vision, multiracial people too can know their own lives as a Christophany and, in so doing, discover new and empowered ways to navigate racialized experiences in the world. For example, they may learn to identify race and multiraciality as an important aspect of their *identification*, and yet reconciling their racial identification through touching it from

72. Raimon Panikkar, *Christophany: The Fullness of Man* (Maryknoll, NY: Orbis Books, 2004), 189.

73. Panikkar, *Cultures and Religions in Dialogue, Part One,* 1.

their deeper Christophanic *identity*. Though multiraciality is an important social construct and context for the ways that a person engages with the world, a person's Christophany is their awareness of themselves as interdependent with Life itself, as not reducible to any one label, category, or aspect of experience. To develop a practical theology of multi/racial experience(s), I argue that we must weave experiences of the ongoing and dynamic racial status of mixed-race people through their deepest spiritual knowing, what Panikkar calls Christophany.

A practical theology of multi/racial experience(s), then, is a mystically informed invitation for multiracial people to engage critically and compassionately with their racialized experiences from a place of inner clarity. I refer to this as the experience of Multiracial Christophany. Multiracial Christophany as a spiritual vision carries four movements within it that were birthed from the process of cross-fertilization between the spiritual themes of multiraciality (from chapter 2) and the four aspects relating to each of them in Panikkar's life (previously noted in this chapter). These four movements are the foundations of the new spiritual formation program that I created to foster intergenerational connections, inclusive care, integral creativity, and interdependent communion. Because the next chapter explores this program in practice, I conclude this chapter by attending to these four movements in more detail.

Intergenerational Connection

Finding rootedness within tradition(s) is a vital aspect of Multiracial Christophany. Above, I mentioned that Panikkar was heavily grounded in his roots flowing from the archetype of the monk as well as through the example of contemplatives who lived before him. Each of these two "roots" allowed Panikkar to find spiritual ancestors and a living tradition that spoke to his life in all its particularities and encouraged him to become uniquely transparent to Divine Mystery. Panikkar did not romanticize their examples but found support in them to live more fully alive as his unique self, in solidarity with the whole of Life.

Multiracial people profoundly need the radical remembrance of those who have gone before us because historical and contemporary structural oppressions continue to erase or dismiss our memories and stories of ancestors. Even in the rare cases where these ancestors are remembered, such memories can be for the purposes of domination and preservation of the illusion of racial purity; this includes the horrors, violence, evil, and "impurity" that multiraciality represents. Multiracial Christophany speaks to the need to recover "roots" that have been lost and then how to transgress boundaries by embodying love that integrates new ways of spiritual being and knowing. Recovering these roots will reveal intergenerational sources of replenishment and restoration for the many nuances and diverse realities of multi/racial experience(s).

Inclusive Care

Inclusive care is a second movement of Multiracial Christophany. Inclusive care takes its lead from Panikkar's contemplative mood as a new attitude that welcomes the dynamisms of life nonjudgmentally so that previously unimagined possibilities can be explored. Raimon Panikkar expressed an attitude of nonattachment to fixed realities and a rejection of monolithic ethnocentrisms of all kinds. He wrote, "Let my identity grow so I may be able to identify with my body and with all the earth and at the same time distance myself from everything and not absolutize anything."[74] Panikkar committed his life to the contemplative mood that does not over-identify with any one aspect of reality but sees reality itself, including his own experiences, as pluralistic. "Cosmotheandric" was his description of the mystical experience he perceived as moving in continuous triadic and relational flow. In Panikkar's contemplative vision, he rejected hierarchies of injustice and instead favored an all-inclusive attitude that does not impose any one definition on the whole of Life. Panikkar advocated that multidimensional relationships of reciprocity be cultivated so that differences can be accepted through love. Panikkar's contemplative attitude is apt for multiracial people who seek to embrace the plurality of their own ethnic and cultural heritage, and in turn multiracial people can begin to identify how being "mixed" can be a blessing toward reconciliation amid the increasing fissures of racialized societies.

Multiracial Christophany calls for an embrace of the unique microcosm of each person which holistically reflects the macrocosm of reality itself. It is a posture of inclusive care that combats the (distorted) attitudes of felt inferiority to those the dominant society deems as "racially pure," resulting in the burden of monoracial normativity placed on multi/racial experience(s).[75] A new movement of inclusive care encourages a curious approach to diversity, first within the interiority of each person and then second within Reality at large. Furthermore, inclusive care encourages multiracial people to experience differences as additions to life rather than "impurities" to be cast out. If multiracial people are encouraged to embrace the many aspects of who they are, I contend that such a mysti-

74. Panikkar, *The Water of the Drop*, 318.

75. Distorted attitudes are one of the four essential themes I have identified as important in multi/racial experience(s) from the previous chapter.

cism can also invite monoracial persons to overcome their own patterns of racialization and instead move toward a realization of Christophany. The movement of inclusive care asks each person to welcome their full selves into the spaces and communities they occupy and to resist monolithic or hegemonic constructions of self-awareness.

Integral Creativity

Integral creativity is a third movement of Multiracial Christophany. Moving from an attitude of inclusive care, integral creativity is the participatory action of loving relationship with Reality so that Reality can be renewed continually.[76] Creative action is at the heart of Panikkar's interculturality as it stemmed from his belief that Life is always being (re)created and the human vocation is to co-author Life alongside all other beings. Panikkar modeled his own creative action by emphasizing the power of Resurrection Life as the mystical awareness of life as continuous and ever-new flow. Such a posture is profoundly creative yet risky because it knows that Life is unpredictable and can neither be tamed nor manipulated at will. Integral creativity is a stark rejection of the technocratic civilization that is proliferated through the propaganda of empires, social media, and popular culture because of the receptive listening that undergirds it. For multi/racial experience(s) that seek spiritual well-being today, Panikkar invites Life to be fully lived by embracing the radical unknown of each day and participat-

76. I am grateful for the work of Jorge N. Ferrer and Jacob H. Sherman, eds., *The Participatory Turn: Spirituality, Mysticism, Religious Studies* (Albany: State University of New York Press, 2008), who stress the importance of individual and community engagement and how that impacts the ongoing creativity of Life as a whole.

ing in Life's constant interactions. It is through both acceptance of Life as it is as well as engagement with it that creates the path of what Panikkar referred to as "blessed simplicity."[77]

Integral creativity is an emergent, contextual, and adaptive approach from which many multiracial people can benefit as they are constantly forced to navigate racialized dynamics in diverse situations in the world. Panikkar's insistence on living the adventure of Life with cosmic confidence becomes a necessary resource for emergent multiracial spiritualities and reminds racialized persons to make creative choices in dialogue with the harmony of Life. Multiracial Christophany invites those who are multiracial to propel life forward in new and wonderful ways that transcend the limits imposed by race and racial oppression. This does not mean multiracial people are the answer to "race" and its attending problems in and of themselves. Rather, it means that they, too, have distinctive and important contributions that are necessary if collective healing is possible. In this way, the creativity of Multiracial Christophany can heal senses of (*devitalized*) *actions* like the fight, flight, or freeze responses to violence that often stunt racial justice through fear. Rather than having to conform to the social constructs that have been prescribed for them, multiracial people can simultaneously acknowledge their experiences as racialized while also transcending dynamics of racialization through personal awareness of Christophany. This both/and affirmation helps people to deal fully with the realities of race without minimizing or spiritually bypassing them while also witnessing the many gifts and graces that their experiences hold beyond issues of race.

77. Panikkar, *Mysticism and Spirituality, Part Two*, 127.

Interdependent Communion

Interdependent communion is the last movement within Multiracial Christophany and emphasizes the important *associations* that are necessary for mixed-race people. Multiracial Christophany recognizes that no being exists separate from the Whole and, therefore, calls for vitality to be renewed by returning to nourish all the relationships that sustain Life. Multiracial Christophany asks us to reflect consciously on the "who" that makes up our life and become aware of our interdependence with other human beings, the cosmos, and the divine.

Multiracial spiritualities are intuitively multidimensional and polyperspectival because of the vast diversity of their experiences, but Multiracial Christophany asks multiracial people to go beyond connection solely with other mixed-race people (and even beyond human relations alone) and aim at re-establishing connections with the cosmic and divine facets of Reality. To understand this relational approach, recalling Panikkar's linguistic term "ecosophy" is particularly fruitful. With an embrace of interdependence,[78] multiracial people will find community with All Life. A movement of interdependent communion is a powerful corrective for multiracial persons who experience *(debilitated) associations* due to alienation from monoracialized others and/or the estrangement produced by rapid acceleration, speed, and efficiency that has stifled natural cosmic rhythms of rest in our current age of technology. Multiracial Christophany admits that, for healing to come, it must come through reconciled relations and restored communion.

78. Raimon Panikkar came up with the neologism "inter-independence" as a way to emphasize the importance of both particular uniqueness and the interrelatedness of all life. See "Human Dialogue and Religious Inter-Independence: Fire and Crystal," *Faith and Development* (January 2003).

Mysticism, Compassion, and Multiraciality (MCAM): Creating a Spiritual Formation Program for Multiracial Christophany

Following Panikkar, a practical theology of multi/racial experience(s) ought to be the fruit of a life and praxis that attends to the four core movements of Multiracial Christophany. This book, indeed, emerges from the practice of a spiritual formation program that I created called Mysticism, Compassion, and Multiraciality (MCAM). In the next chapter, I discuss MCAM and its practices. Multiracial Christophany enlivens MCAM, and the remainder of this chapter highlights various ways that the connection between the two is significant for mixed-race people.

First, Multiracial Christophany is an experience that is deeply rooted within spirituality and Christianity, but it also transcends the historicity of religion, making more space for its own renewal through relationships with the wisdom of other creatures, cultures, and religions. The ability to both embrace and transcend religious and cultural experiences is vital when creating a program for mixed-race people who live between and beyond monoracial and monocultural ideologies that are the social status quo of North America. Second, Multiracial Christophany seeks to normalize the pluralism of our spiritual journeys and clearly emphasizes that no one culture, religion, group, or language has the solution alone. To accept pluralism, there must also be a commitment to practice nonviolent and compassionate listening within ourselves and toward one another. In short, an intercultural hospitality is the only sustainable way forward. This posture is especially advantageous for multiracial people who often have parents who are from differing religious, ethnic, or cultural backgrounds and who wonder how to assimilate these seemingly divergent realities within their own experience.

Multiracial Christophany centers ways of being that are expansive enough to affirm and respect the irreducibility of differences by not rejecting, minimizing, caricaturing, or homogenizing difference to one meta-religious interpretation—reinscribing the oppressions of colonialism—while also relating in sensitivity to the real diversity of cultures and religious experiences that are not one's own. Third, Multiracial Christophany centers the unique wisdoms that emerge from multiracial people throughout the world. Refusing to be limited to abstraction, Multiracial Christophany encourages mixed-race people to pay attention to lived experiences for the purposes of becoming more conscious participants who heal the division, fragmentation, and polarization that increasingly characterize human societies and relations in the world.

Multiracial Christophany is a radical and spiritually oriented way of tending to suffering in the world, particularly racialized experiences, and race-based oppression. Furthermore, it is a contemporary way of living out Panikkar's insistence on metanoia, what he describes as a "circumcision of the mind, that transcends the nous"[79] and disrupts neatly prescribed racial categories inherited from dominant (monocultural) ideologies.[80] I see this work as a direct response to Panikkar's realization that peace is walked out at many levels, personally and relationally, "not through the tower of Babel, but by building well-paved roads from house to house."[81] The prominence of pluralism within the life of Panikkar's own ancestry is an essential starting point for developing practical theologies that can inculcate emergent multiracial spiritualities in depth and breadth, so that

79. Panikkar, *Mysticism and Spirituality, Part One,* xxi.

80. Panikkar, *Christianity, Part Two,* 24.

81. Nihun Mehta, "Compassion as a Basic Global Ethic | ServiceSpace. Org," August 31, 2014.

the many particularities of lived experiences will be cherished and honored.

Mysticism, Compassion, and Multiraciality, then, constitute a new spiritual formation program focusing on multi/racial experience(s) so that participants can cultivate community and find empowerment in the work of racial, intercultural, and cosmic justice. The program also provides critical spiritual accompaniment to multiracial people as they experience the infinite value of their lives even while the inner and outer turmoil of racialization persists. MCAM encourages courageous social action to be discerned collectively as to resist the individualizing tendencies of colonization, racism, and internalized oppression. Guiding questions that animated the creation of the program were practical and included the following: What are the best ways to support mixed-race people as they tend to racialized experiences? What new spiritual paradigms must be forged to assist multiracial people to be more intimately and courageously present to their own marginalized multi/racial experience(s) as they sit between cultures, traditions, and social location? What wisdom do multiracial spiritualities offer others who are seeking to better attend to dynamics of race and racial oppression in a pluralistic society? In the chapter that follows, I give a detailed overview of the program as well as initial findings that emerged in consideration of these questions.

3

Transforming Multiraciality through Mysticism: A Critical Evaluation of MCAM

Does my program really make a difference? Is it even helpful? I am not so sure. It might seemingly make things worse. I sure hope not. I want it to be a blessing. When I reflect on my own life and spiritual practice, what I am learning more and more is that sometimes life is mysteriously unexplainable and there is nothing I can do to avoid that. Life is big, expansive, complex, and dynamic. Somehow though, I am a part of it all and it is a part of me. In my stammering, I ask the divine how to live, and the gentle reply is simply: *surrender.* I am invited to become aware how my preoccupation with *thinking* I alone can make something of life is what gives me a burdened heart. I am invited to simply *wait, rest,* and *be.* To be is much more difficult than to do. It requires a letting go, a childlike faith, and a collapse into the mysterious infinity of it all. As weird as it can sound, it is the admission of my own vulnerability and perplexed status of being a finite human that God's love is most deeply revealed. I have come to see that I am loved through and through—even though many contradictory thoughts, emotions, and experiences persist.

This experiential salvation does not lead me to leave behind the cares of life but calls that I venture more deeply into it. There I find a deeper awareness of a Love that is hidden among all things and permeates it to no end. My hope is this program will help cultivate hearts that receive and perceive the divine life that flows in and through all things. I suspect the Spirit will be revealed when least anticipated, but when the Spirit shows up, perhaps the only response will be gratitude. Life is a pure gift indeed. In opening our lives up, and in some cases having it broken open through suffering, we realize ourselves as the fragile yet sacred vessels through whom God's love is being revealed.—*Aizaiah Yong,* journal entry, Los Angeles, CA, 2019

In this chapter, I present a qualitative analysis of the spiritual program that I created based on the theoretical foundations and guiding movements I shared in chapter 3. The program is called Mysticism, Compassion, and Multiraciality (MCAM). I first give an overview of the program, including the week-by-week structure. I then share the process and findings of the qualitative analysis I performed. Finally, I offer recommendations for the future of the program as well as the ways that I feel this work connects to and extends the legacy of Raimon Panikkar.

It is important to restate that I do not attempt to engage multi/racial experience(s) from purely theoretical standpoints. Rather, I sought to join myself (as a multiracial person) to the lives of the participants and accompany them in a facilitator-researcher role,[1] so that the research came directly from those I am seeking to serve. In this spirit, this chapter is filled with many direct quotes from the participants that elucidate my intentions. In structuring the program, I followed the spirit of the "sangama: an experiential small group dialogue form pioneered by Raimon Panikkar," which was a group of people "who don't just 'get together' but 'go together' led by the spirit . . . in a new style of life . . . going deep enough into any topic to touch the core, the Mystery."[2] The overall goal was to cultivate bonds of friendship and companionship that could strengthen foundations of interrelatedness and that, in turn, would create increased mutuality and love. Through this process, I was able to experience more deeply that "Truth is not univocal . . . and cannot be reduced to one concept."[3] My goal as a facilitator was twofold: first, to embody a presence of spacious listening so that equity in sharing could be experienced, and second, to reflect to the group the sacred dimensions that were arising from their authentic sharing. Therefore, in the spirit of friendship and of pluralism, I offer this practical theological analysis, concluding with three affirmations for cultivating compassionate connections to multi/racial experience(s) and three risks to consider when taking a spiritual formation approach to multiraciality.

1. I embraced what Michael Quinn Patton calls a "mini-ethnographer." See *Qualitative Research & Evaluation Methods: Integrating Theory and Practice*, 4th ed. (Thousand Oaks, CA: Sage Publications, 2015).

2. Kate Olson, "Living the New Story," *Fetzer Institute*, 2012, https://fetzer.org.

3. Raimon Panikkar, *Cultures and Religions in Dialogue, Part One: Pluralism and Interculturality*, ed. Milena Carrara Pavan (Maryknoll, NY: Orbis Books, 2014), xiii.

A Programmatic Overview of MCAM

MCAM was a virtual, four-week spiritual formation program in which each participant was invited to connect to their own experiences of racialization in the United States by way of mysticism and spirituality. While the program has roots in Christian mysticism,[4] the program did not explicitly use Christian Scripture or language or require a background in mysticism or spirituality. Rather, MCAM sought to facilitate and strengthen relationships within the multiracial population (and then extend to Life as a Whole) through shared teaching and practices related to critical race studies, mysticism, compassion, and intercultural dialogue. It was also clear that the purpose of the program was to "go together" so that, in our bonds of solidarity, new resources would emerge to enable us all to better attend to the socio-political and racialized dynamics that multiracial people face in the United States. MCAM assumed that liberating power is discovered when presence and attention are offered to the lives and spiritualities of mixed-race people and additionally that the insights offered from multiraciality are not only beneficial for multiracial people, but for all people who are seeking to resist racism. I see my assumption in alignment with Raimon Panikkar's belief that social oppression and centuries of colonization must be overcome through mystical experience and the rejection of monolithic and monocultural categories.[5] Therefore, the program was created to support myself and seven

4. The program marketing material was created by the generosity and creativity of Alyssa Simonson, whom I give thanks for. The PDF announcement made clear that the program did not seek to convert them to Christianity (or any religion) and was shared via social media, email invitation, and a few flyers for distribution during in-person events.

5. Panikkar called this "cultural disarmament." See "Books: Cultural Disarmament," Fundació Vivarium Raimon Panikkar, 2022.

other participants in a journey together, contemplating more fully the multifaceted and intersectional experiences of multiraciality with the hopes of promoting the spiritual well-being of North American life at large.

The makeup of the program included "four components of praxis" that are generally common in spiritual formation across North America including plenary teaching, introspection through journaling, group dialogue, and guided meditation.[6] Each of these four components, however, were approached through Raimon Panikkar's unique Cosmotheandric Vision, fostering awareness of Life in its triadic structure. While I did not explicitly refer to his practice of intrareligious dialogue or his spiritual vision of Christophany or cosmotheandrism to the participants, I instead referred to him as a foundational teacher from whom the program was created. The aim of the program was to support participants in an integral and transformational spiritual posture[7] toward their racialized experiences, allowing for transformation that expands capacities of hospitality to all that is different. The approach of MCAM was in direct opposition to a systematic[8] or Eurocentric approach to spirituality, which seeks primarily to compare, contrast, and essentialize differences.[9]

The program met synchronously, once per week, online, where I led them through teaching, facilitated dialogue around lived

6. Eric J. Kyle, *Living Spiritual Praxis: Foundations for Spiritual Formation Program Development* (Eugene, OR: Pickwick Publications, 2013), 60.

7. Panikkar describes this as "metanoia," which arises from spiritual practice, wisdom, and authentic cross-fertilization. See *Mysticism and Spirituality, Part One: Mysticism, the Fullness of Life*, ed. Milena Carrara Pavan (Maryknoll, NY: Orbis Books, 2014), xxi.

8. See Kyle, *Living Spiritual Praxis.*

9. Elizabeth Conde-Frazier, S. Steve Kang, and Gary A. Parrett, *A Many Colored Kingdom: Multicultural Dynamics for Spiritual Formation* (Grand Rapids, MI: Baker Academic, 2004).

experiences of multiraciality, and guided meditation. The participants understood that the spiritual formation program was designed not simply to acquire more information but to receive and participate in Life's transformation inter-in-dependently,[10] that together we would experience and embody the presence of peacemaking in the world.

MCAM was a novel attempt to create a spiritual formation program that centered multi/racial experience(s) and was hosted completely online. The program created an opportunity for multiracial people to affirm the multiplicity and plurality of mixed-race heritage and unashamedly strengthen capacities of resistance to the oppressive powers of colonialism that deem others outside the dominant group as "inferior." The following sections briefly summarize the contents of each week.

Introductory Session: Week 1

In the first week, my main goal was to establish connection, community, and confidence in the overall group dynamics. Knowing that trust is imperative when inviting people to share from and in their spiritual lives, I emailed a prompt to participants in advance of our first live synchronous gathering. My email served to reassure participants of what to expect for the first session and offered them a prompt to reflect on if they wanted to prepare in advance for our session together. In the first gathering, I sought to create opportunities for participants to authentically highlight the uniqueness of their experiences, to speak to spirituality as they understood it, and to share aloud

10. Inter-in-dependence is a phrase that Panikkar would use to describe the ways in which uniqueness does not disappear in the spiritual life, but neither does it result in individualism. Life is all interwoven. See Raimon Panikkar, "Human Dialogue and Religious Inter-Independence: Fire and Crystal," *Faith and Development*, January 2003.

any questions they were bringing to the group specifically pertaining to multiraciality. The last of these three opportunities was a significant chance for participants in the group to connect with others' conscious or unconscious racialized experiences.

The prompt that participants came prepared to share asked the participants to briefly state five things: the history of their full name;[11] something unique to their experience of which they are proud; their self-understanding of their racial identification along with any other aspects of their identity they desired to disclose; what drew them to participate in the program; and a question or hope they had for their engagement. Throughout the session, I emphasized that this would likely be the first time that they would have been part of a group that focused explicitly on multi/racial experience(s) and so to exercise as much self and other compassion as possible. Furthermore, this group would be an opportunity to relate to one another from the depth dimension of our innermost being, rather than just our logical and rational minds. The North American preoccupation with and training toward the logical and rational mind, then, was to be approached without assuming it was supremely important for our multi/racial experience(s).

The group agreed to nurture a supportive environment for one another that fostered sharing transparently from the core of our experiences, relating to one another in nonjudgmental curiosity amid our differences, and seeking to repair relations with one another if offense took place. The group also ensured a certain level of safety with one another by agreeing to hold strict

11. As critical race studies attests, it is essential for BIPOC communities to recover and reclaim the use of original names in public settings as this empowers the personal sense of agency and resists names given to those who have been minoritized only for the purposes of making comfortable those in the dominant culture. See Rita Kohli and Daniel G. Solórzano, "Teachers, Please Learn Our Names! Racial Microaggressions and the K–12 Classroom," *Race Ethnicity and Education* 15, no. 4 (September 2012): 441–62.

confidentiality, understanding that, if at any time, a member would not like to participate, they had the freedom to withdraw from participation.

I began the time of sharing by going first and then invited the next person (and so on and so on). I dedicated almost the entirety of the first session to holding space for each person to be honored, celebrated, and encouraged in their sharing. Near the end of the session, I led them in a short meditation on their experiences of embodiment as constituted by the generosity of the four elements that make up the cosmos.[12] Each participant was able to take a moment and reflect on how the practice landed with them, and I ended with a benediction that included a call to more conscious living supported by a quotation of Raimon Panikkar: "The real criterion of true contemplation is that it leads to praxis, even if that praxis consists only in transforming one's own life and immediate environment."[13]

Contemplating Racialized Bodies: Week 2

The second week focused on inviting a deepening awareness of rootedness in the many relations that support each person—the self, others, institutions, the divine, and the cosmos. In preparation for our time, I asked participants to read a small excerpt from Frank Rogers's book *Practicing Compassion*.[14] Rogers emphasizes care at the center of thriving relationships, and

12. The elements I focused on are connected to Panikkar's Quaternitas Perfecta: air, wind, fire, and water. See chap. 14 in Raimon Panikkar, *Mysticism and Spirituality, Part Two: Spirituality, the Way of Life*, ed. Milena Carrara Pavan (Maryknoll, NY: Orbis Books, 2014).

13. Fred Dallmayr quotes Panikkar in his chapter "Sacred Secularity and Prophetism: A Tension in Panikkar's Work?," in Peter C. Phan and Young-chan Ro, eds., *Raimon Panikkar: A Companion to His Life and Thought* (Cambridge, UK: James Clarke, 2018), 240.

14. Frank Rogers Jr., *Practicing Compassion* (Nashville, TN: Upper Room, 2015), 35–40.

the excerpt accompanied a video of Raimon Panikkar's "The Window,"[15] which helped lay a foundation for understanding the spiritual value of each experience for the Whole. Together, these two primers emphasized listening to one another's diverse perspectives as central in our healing work.

In the live synchronous session, I began with a plenary teaching introducing them to the Buddhist notion of interdependence. I then made connections to this notion of interdependence and showed how it is something not exclusive to Buddhism but also discussed in other religious traditions, emphasizing the big idea that nothing in life exists on its own. I shared how some might understand this reality to be thanks to the generosity and goodness of the divine and others claim to know it as simply a fact of life through observation. I invited the participants to become more aware of interdependence through a practice of bringing to attention spontaneous moments of joy and delight in their day and week and tracing those moments to a relationship that allowed them to happen.[16] A second invitation followed, evoking interdependence as real by focusing on a time of precarity in their lives such as moments of suffering or powerlessness. As in the first reflection, the participants were encouraged to trace those moments to notice relationships coming to provide care and support to them in the midst of difficulty and hardship. Further illustrating precarity, I shared my own experience of compassion from cosmic elements, other human beings, and the divine after surviving a near-death motorcycle accident.

15. Stillpoint: The Center for Christian Spirituality, "Raimon Panikkar: The Window," video (September 5, 2015); www.youtube.com.

16. My foundations for this come from James Finley's invitation to tend to trauma from the contemplative dimensions of "spontaneous spiritual experience," which he details in his Transforming Trauma recordings available on his website. See James Finley, "Transforming Trauma Recordings," 2009, https://jamesfinley.org/ish.

I concluded the time by reviewing a brief history of multiraciality in the United States, defining "race" and "racism" along with other important terms, and especially highlighting the imperative to move beyond the North American (and post–civil rights era) attitude of colorblindness. In the historical and critical review, participants learned about MultiCrit, and they were given the opportunity to respond with their personal experiences of oppression internally, interpersonally, and structurally as multiracial people. The invitation was to reflect on how spirituality was or was not experientially felt in these moments. We ended the session in a shared, guided meditation that helped to expand awareness of compassion as the guiding force of all our relations.

Extending Compassion toward Multi/racial Experience(s) of Others: Week 3

In the third week, the participants were asked to dialogue with others in the group and listen to the racialized experiences of others, practicing compassionate listening to these experiences within themselves. The goal was to develop attitudes of ever-expanding hospitality and openness to the world around us that can be strengthened by the divine feminine.[17] To set the stage, I began the plenary time by leading the participants in a practice of receiving sacred compassion from the earth. I then taught the theory of intersectionality, showing how each person's multiracial experience is unique, depending on their racial heritage and other social identities.[18] I stressed that harmony and peace

17. I am grateful for Raimon Panikkar's insistence on the recovery of "Yin" as essential to our healing and social engagement. See his discussion of this in Panikkar, *Mysticism and Spirituality, Part Two,* 29–32.

18. Following my discussion of intersectionality previously in chap. 2, other important factors of one's social location include their political identifi-

could not be realized through force, will, or the homogenization of experiences. Each of us, therefore, is called to make space within ourselves that can embrace the various aspects of our own (and others') experience(s). Making such a space is a profoundly spiritual posture to the world that may or may not have been consistent with the religious spaces that participants had been a part of before. I encouraged the group to be careful, patient, and curious, inviting them to honor, validate, and affirm the truth and suffering of others.

Before I broke them up into pairs, I led them in a brief, guided breath meditation. The participants experienced each breath as a gift of Life, giving itself to us without judgment and without restraint. I invited them, situated in the generosity of our breathing and our bodies, to welcome awareness of the many identities and social locations that are present in the experiences of others. I then asked them to consider how compassion might be a resource for each of them to be more fully present in their relationships with others and their racialized experiences—a gentle spirit, perhaps a courageous action, words of affirmation, or helping a person leave the situation to find safety. The session ended with a group sharing time of what they learned through compassionate listening and how they can apply it in their everyday life.

Extending Compassion toward Difficult Others: Week 4

In the final week, we focused on discerning new actions that we might take as we move away from the program. Some of the questions that we considered were:

cation, spiritual affiliation, gender, sexual orientation, socio-economic status, ability, citizenship, language, etc.

What in the program impacted you?
What in the program challenged you?
What insights were received in the program?
What creative opportunities lie ahead beyond the program?

I contextualized these questions with a presentation on the connections between a compassionate approach to racism and the Gandhian notion of *satyagraha*. Translated as "truth-force," one who practices *satyagraha* resists evil nonviolently and works for evil to be transformed into the highest good that includes all people, even oppressors.[19] I reassured the participants that compassionate practice in the world is not about being nice or soft but is a way of being that embodies courageous, prophetic, and spiritually rooted action,[20] and did this by differentiating what I call *unwise* compassion from *wise* compassion.

Unwise compassion uses the language of compassion as the rationale to bypass the reality of having to deal with evil by either minimizing it or trying to escape it. *Wise* compassion, by contrast, is not a result of human willpower or effort alone but emerges from mystical experience in which one knows compassion is at the heart of life and present amid the most difficult pains of humanity. An attitude of *wise* compassion refuses to dehumanize or demonize others but instead speaks and lives the truth, calling and inviting forth a higher way of being in the world.[21] The practice of *wise* compassion also does not impose

19. Michael J. Nojeim, *Gandhi and King: The Power of Nonviolent Resistance* (Westport, CT: Praeger, 2004).

20. Aizaiah G. Yong, "Decolonizing Pastoral Care in the Classroom: An Invitation to a Pedagogy of Spirit Experience," *Teaching Theology & Religion* 24, no. 2 (June 2021): 107–16, https://doi.org/10.1111/teth.12585.

21. I am building upon what Raimon Panikkar described in his journal entry on the action of prayer as not an escape from the world but paradoxically about "transcending and deepening processes." See entry from August 3, 1971, in Raimon Panikkar, *The Water of the Drop: Fragments from Pan-*

certain behaviors on others but offers the visibility of their own humanity (and the embrace of finitude) as a way of inviting those who do harm to choose to live differently. Finally, I presented the idea that *wise* compassion is a way of living that is empowered, centered, and consciously aware of the possible risks of their action, yet chooses to do so in love anyway. Wise compassion is not realized as an individual who acts separately from the whole of life. Rather, it emerges from the spiritual knowing of one's identity as interwoven with all of Life. As an alternative to the oppressions of modern individualism, a spirituality that empowers interweaving love as the basis of all our relations reorients action in ways that are transformative at the deepest levels. I then reminded the participants of the words of Thomas Merton, who said our activism must "not depend on the hope of results."[22] Instead, hope is a reality in the deepest dimensions of Life and experientially gives us the strength to suffer for, with, and for the sake of the world as it is transformed by love.

Again drawing on Panikkar's intuition regarding the connection between praxis and contemplation, I invited the participants to move beyond my presentation and practice compassionate connection in a guided meditation. They were invited to remember someone with whom they had experienced a difficult racialized encounter, not necessarily someone they might consider to be "an enemy," but someone with whom they did not easily feel sympathy.[23] For many of the participants, this

ikkar's Diaries (Delhi: Indian Society for Promoting Christian Knowledge, 2018), 74.

22. Thomas Merton, "Thomas Merton's Letter to a Young Activist—Jim and Nancy Forest," https://jimandnancyforest.com/2014/10/mertons-letter-to-a-young-activist/.

23. This particular practice was an adaption of Frank Rogers's "practicing compassion with a difficult other." See Rogers, *Practicing Compassion,* 81–104.

was their first time practicing a compassionate connection with someone who has been the target of their harbored anger or resentment, so the meditation ended with sharing in the joys and challenges of practicing compassion in this community.

The fourth session was the final session of the program, so it was important to conclude it with shared spiritual practice. We concluded our time together with a communal practice of discernment, bringing to bear our deepest transformations from the program. I asked the participants to focus on any one of the four natural elements of the earth that they feel they needed most now, to feel it in their bodies, and to more fully receive the gift and power that the element offers to their nourishment.[24] I invited them to savor the qualitative energy of the element they chose and to imagine radiating that energy to all of Life. I then asked the participants to imagine what it would be like to tap into these gifts and qualities so that, from these foundations, they could act courageously to transform racism and racial oppression. We closed by each sharing one word aloud that will guide and ground them to be more fully engaged in and with the world in each moment.

Findings of MCAM

I am overwhelmingly grateful for the people who participated in this program and the ways that their lives have profoundly impacted me. I set out to encourage them and offer spiritual support to them as they navigated their own multi/racial experience(s), but I received so much more than I gave. The group shared authentically, courageously, and beautifully their

24. This practice was created from the wisdom of Brother Ishmael Tetteh, whom I was blessed to know as a spiritual retreat leader in 2019. See his teaching "Nature as a Teacher with Brother Ishmael Tetteh," episode of *Life Conversations,* with Life Coach Ade, Blog Talk Radio, 2012.

own lives, spiritualities, and longings to see the world heal. It is my honor to present their wisdom in this chapter and throughout this book. The purpose of this book is to develop a practical theology of multi/racial experience(s), and their contributions I bore witness to through MCAM have been critical in this process. These contributions, often in the form of direct quotes from participants in the study, disclose my broader findings about and analysis of MCAM. By centering the experiences of the participating practitioners of MCAM, the remainder of this chapter demonstrates vital lived aspects of what the theories of critical mixed-race studies, practical theologies of race, and cosmotheandric mysticism have attempted to recount yet in critically new and important ways. I present my overall findings in three main sections: Risks Inherent to MCAM, Affirmations of MCAM, and Future Possibilities of Transforming MCAM.

Risks Inherent to MCAM

Mysticism, Compassion, and Multiraciality is a critically important tool for undergirding the necessary anti-racist work in North American communities with spiritual awareness and courage. MCAM is not, however, without risk. Throughout the practice, participants identified four risks that are inherent to MCAM and that demand care-filled attention from people who seek to approach multiraciality through mysticism and spirituality. The four risks are the prevalence of mixed-race denial, racial trauma, the insistence of individualism, and lack of social support.

The prevalence of mixed-race denial is a persistent pattern and problem in contemporary US settings. Furthermore, MCAM identified patterns that are especially present in predominantly white and Christian settings. Many of the participants were instructed throughout their religiously based and societally racialized upbringing that race was not ultimately important and so to assume a perspective of colorblindness. Obviously, this is a contradictory and confusing rationale that simultaneously communicates the "unimportance" of race yet prescribing a very specific racialized way to engage themselves and the world—through colorblindness. The vicious cycle of colorblindness creates fertile ground for the denial of their own racialized experiences and then is perpetuated and reified through religious or spiritual justifications. Relatedly, for almost all participants, MCAM was the first opportunity they have had to learn about critical mixed-race theory and to reflect on it with others who are supportive and identify as multiracial. It was clear that none of the participants in MCAM had been given adequate opportunities to understand their own racialization in their upbringing and that this reality resulted in spiritual harm. While participants felt the impact of the denial of their mixed-race identities differently, the result was the same: race-based pain and exclusion.

After the program, one participant, Molly,[25] shared that she had grown accustomed to shutting down internally if race was brought up because she knew her experience was different from that of monoracial others and was often dismissed by them. "When something uncomfortable happens regarding my multiraciality," she noted, "I usually just let it go and forget about it." She expressed sadness about this and longed to be in more conversations with other multiracial people who could help her heal and better understand her experience.

In her pre-program interview, Faye, another participant, shared that conversations about race usually end up making her feel awkward and unable to connect with others because of the

25. All quotes are taken from participant interviews with the author in keeping with the study guidelines; see Appendixes for further information on the structure of the study.

ways she has repeatedly been misunderstood. "I feel like I haven't really liked to talk about [race] in a group setting, because I just know where race is at right now; it has become more of a political conversation, and I just don't want to do that with people that I'm not extremely comfortable with," she said. Her response to regularly being misunderstood has been to avoid discussing race altogether, which consequently has done even more damage to her. She noticed that, socially, "no one wants to go there or be that person to bring it up, so I just don't either. I think this is probably part of the problem," as she expresses her growing awareness that ignoring racialization negatively impacts multi/racial experience(s).

In the group setting of MCAM, Brooklyn shared that she worries about being perceived as aggressive if she speaks her truth about race. "I am not a very confrontational person, personality-wise, and so, I try to not be aggressive when we talk about race or anything revolving around race . . . because I know that everybody has a different opinion." Brooklyn recognized that race denial can serve as a short-term self-protection mechanism, and as she noted in some instances, "oftentimes, I don't share." Here is an example of how reinforcing the racist goal of denying her own racialized experiences may provide temporary protection but leaves her feeling invisible and further marginalized, even among racially minoritized populations.

While I began the program with the correct assumption that many people have had negative racialized experiences because of their multiracial identity, I was not prepared for the fact that *all* of the participants would enter the program without any history of substantial discussion on multi/racial experience(s) *at all.* The only conversations they had were dismissive and lacked care. The prevalence of mixed-race denial in society has left multiracial populations with a huge lack of access to nurturing spaces that can promote racial justice. Therefore, mixed-race denial is a reality that should be stated and normalized from the beginning of any discussions on race and racism when considering multiracial people. In doing so, participants will be allowed to realize that their experiences are real, and this can open a door to healing past experiences of shame and exclusion that they have experienced for so long.

Furthermore, the prevalence of mixed-race denial in society means that MCAM needs to introduce critical mixed-race theory at a beginner's level and cannot assume that participants have any background understanding the persistence of race, racial oppression, and monoracism in their communities. Perhaps an effective way to approach CMRS at such an introductory level would be to spend less time on theory and more time on story telling. Additionally, due to the reality of how little validation mixed-race people have experienced, it is vital that group dynamics be created wherein participants know that they will be respected, validated, affirmed, and celebrated for whatever experiences they choose to bring to the table.

Another key risk to MCAM is the reality of racial trauma that participants bring with them into the program. In the qualitative analysis of the program, I found that all participants had many experiences of micro- and macroaggressions in which they were otherized and marginalized due to their multiraciality. Story after story emerged about how their multiracial status was used to exploit, discount, or silence their voices and perspectives. As I expected, if the subject of race ever did come up in these multiracial people's backgrounds, it was usually in the context of being objectified through the question, "*What* are you?"[26] Because it forgets that each person is a "who," this

26. This question is similar to what is asked of many other multiracial people. See Jillian Paragg, "'What Are You?' Mixed Race Responses to the Racial Gaze," *Ethnicities* 17, no. 3 (2017): 277–98.

question has evoked a variety of responses from mixed-race people. Sometimes, responses include attempts to re-humanize themselves and interrogate back, as in the example of "what do you think I am?"; other times, there is no response, and mixed-race people leave the encounter with deep sadness and hurt. The experience of repeated questioning takes place in almost all social settings: when they are with one of their parents, at their jobs, and when they are in interracial settings.

Ellie shared that she can feel the conversation coming even without looking at the questioner. "I have heard so many times, 'What are you?' I tell them, and they respond, 'Well, I just thought white; I could not see other things.'" Ellie's example shows the monoracist pattern of erasure that renders her experience invisible. Ellie responds amicably yet is forced to educate the monoracial other: "Oh yeah, my dad is white. But my mom is Hispanic. I am Puerto Rican and Costa Rican and Irish, German, and Italian." Instead of embracing Ellie's multiplicity, she is reduced to an odd and unrecognizable mixture. Ellie further described interactions in which coworkers in a predominantly monoracial group (this group in particular is also a racial minority in the United States) would often say, "Oh my God, you are a mutt!" in response to her mixed-race identity. And Ellie said back sadly, "It's usually people who are not mixed that say that."

Faye also described how she felt the impact of being racially profiled in traumatizing ways. Recently she was asked about her ethnicity by a monoracial Chinese coworker, and Faye turned the question around, asking, "What do you think I am?" Her coworker thought that Faye "was Mexican, maybe Native American." When Faye told her that she was Mexican and Chinese, the coworker exclaimed, "Oh, I never would have guessed you were Chinese! You're so dark!" For Faye, experiences like this are important as they are "little things that take a toll." Faye recognized the frequency of these "little things" and the weight of the "toll," noting that "growing up in a white community [led to] hurt and pain . . . from being excluded and often subtly ridiculed for being racially different from them." These memories bear on her posture in the present. "It's hard to look around in the present time and think of the past and have patience and compassion. I understand why a lot of people don't talk about it, because there probably is a lot of hurt that people just suppress," she said. These hurts are buried deep and are directly related to her racialized experiences. "Unlike Martin Luther [King], I have anger, and I have negative sentiments toward white people due to this . . . it's hard not to feel resentment and anger"; Faye's racial trauma is felt through her body language and tone of voice when she reflects on these incidents.

In Molly's case, although she was often asked about her racial identity, she would usually answer "Asian" simply because that is what's outwardly most visible and because she feared judgment in being mixed. "When people [who are not multiracial] ask me what I am, why do I only say Filipino, instead of saying I'm half-Filipino or something like that? Why do I have to suppress the other half of who I am just because of history or whatever is convenient for them?" she asked. Molly has grown tired of feeling the need to always advocate for her own experience just so that she can embrace her full identity. The experience of not being believed or trusted by monoracial people was not unique to Molly.

Will articulated a sense of insecurity and self-doubt because "it is hard to have confidence about race." Will said, "When I was younger, I didn't know if I should be trying to act a certain way or if I should be trying to fit into a certain identity. I wasn't confident at all, so I would have just kind of shut down and kind of take it just to be accepted." The theme of self-suppression in response to racial trauma is evidence of Will's observation that "when conversations become about race, it's dangerous." Blaire's experience was not dissimilar. "I think when race is openly discussed," Blaire said, "it's frightening . . . it brings dissent. And when people are scared, they can get angry or act out." Blaire stated that such fear-rooted responses can split all kinds of social relationships and have devastating effects on mixed-race people. More broadly, "in society, when we talk about race," Blaire noted, "it can be very dangerous and it can strip . . . humanity out . . . very easily. I have seen this."

The participants demonstrated many ways that multiracial people are always having to navigate racial trauma as they are continually fetishized, tokenized, or exoticized by monoracial others. This further complicates how multiracial people either engage or disengage from conversations on race, and it was evident in the ways many participants entered MCAM with a caution and fear that the program might result in a similar outcome. And so, through the insights of these participants, I came to a better understanding of the severity of racialized suffering that accumulates in the lives of multiracial people. This is a serious and real risk to the program that must be tended to delicately and with patience. Because race is such a loaded and sensitive topic, there are ways that participants could easily feel misunderstood or threatened by the program or other participants' framing. Even in a case where a person is relatively open and courageous enough to discuss race more deeply, unexpected discomfort can accompany this work. This program should not replace therapy or other modes of healing that can assist people in processing trauma. I recommend that it be the responsibility of the facilitator to be prepared to refer participants to mental health professionals whose work is also informed by racial trauma, as needed.

Another way to mitigate the risks of racial trauma would be to begin each session with the reminder that participants may or may not be ready for all that will be discussed. Therefore, the imperative is to invite each person to hold a nonjudgmental posture toward themselves and compassionately accept wherever they are at. Given the importance of practicing nonviolence through self-compassion, this option cannot be understated and is one of the greatest resources to respond to this risk.[27] A call for self-compassion creates an open and invitational feel to my program so that participants realize that there are no right or wrong answers and that this journey of healing requires patience. Rather than focusing solely on information, strategies, and quick solutions, the program should place priority on building capacities of generosity and kindness toward oneself, realizing that honesty and sincerity are integral to the group's well-being.

A third risk that became clear in the evaluation of MCAM was the need to consistently resist individualistic understandings of racism and race as an essentialized identity. Multiple times, participants shared how race, racism, and especially monoracism could not be overcome unless it was dealt with dynamically, situationally, holistically, spiritually, and institutionally.

For Sean, the program taught him how vital it is that the educational system learn how to structurally deal with racism and the importance of creating affinity groups that support multiracial people at the institutional level. Creating groups to support multiracial people in response to structural racism would be particularly important in "at-risk schools," he noted.

27. My bias toward self-compassion and its relationship to sustainable social transformation is indebted to the work of Frank Rogers Jr., who wrote a timely piece entitled "Warriors of Compassion: Coordinates on the Compass of Compassion-Based Activism," in Jennifer Baldwin, ed., *Taking It to the Streets: Public Theologies of Activism and Resistance* (Lanham, MD: Lexington Books, 2019), 25–42.

"I could see how much effect it could have on children who are at risk and don't have places to talk about their own experiences of race," Sean said. Such groups, he expressed, would also create space for students "to experience compassion on a personal level." Like Sean, Molly also recognized how narratives of individualism and racial oppression were entwined in educational spaces. "I really like the idea about creating a space where multiracial people can share their experience and learn from one another. At my college," she said, "it would be helpful for my campus to have a space specifically for multiracial people to initiate these conversations." By giving voice to the communal alternative, participants identified the risk of individualism in the face of racism. Unless there is institutional support for creating a safer and more inclusive campus community, efforts for racial justice carried out by individuals can go only so far.

Because the program was small and done outside of their institutions, the participants left the program feeling inspired to imagine structural changes that impact the institutions of which they are a part. Blaire shared her desire to gather "with other multiracial people to talk about their experiences but to also learn the basic language and tools for discussing race in a productive and compassionate manner. Coming together with the support of a trained facilitator is a great way to take action." Blaire clearly understood the need to emphasize that racism and racial oppression are structural realities that can be resisted and transformed only through spiritual wisdom. Doing so empowers participants to "lift up work such as nonfiction, art, music, etc. done by multiracial people" in response to "when others ask or talk about race." Again, the collective alternative demonstrates the individualist risk. "I think collectively lifting up the voices of those who have similar experiences and getting others to engage with them as well can be incredibly powerful," Blaire shared.

A way to manage this risk (and begin to address it) could be to introduce the metaphor of breathing. In the act of breathing, we can experience that life happens not of our own making but rather as received in partnership with the relations of Life itself. We did not choose to start our own breathing, and we cannot choose when to stop it (at least not for long!). In this metaphor, we notice the role of the *in*-breath, showing the importance of tending to our inner worlds by establishing care and connection. However, the *in*-breath by itself is not life; it requires the *out*-breath. We breathe in, and we also breathe out; and that is the generative and restorative action we take (and receive from others as they breathe out) in the outer world. In other words, our spiritual lives cannot remain closed inward but are realized through the flow back and forth. In the spirit of the in-breath, MCAM can facilitate introspection and tender, lovingkindness to the various facets of racialized experiences. However, in the spirit of the out-breath, the program can encourage new social and institutional spaces to be fostered where others can heal from the effects of racism and co-create new possibilities together. MCAM not only leads people to the awareness of the preciousness of their own personal lives but attempts to help them recognize how social systems and structures might be transformed. In this sense, we cannot live out spiritual vitality without attending to both the inner and outer dimensions of Life as well as the ways that race and racism distort Life.

A fourth risk that became apparent through the qualitative analysis of MCAM was the importance of ongoing social support and the potential loss of it after the program ended. MCAM was able to provide a powerful intimate community for the four weeks that it lasted, but it was clear that participants were unsure how they would be sustained in this work without continued community support because of the various ways in which race and racism are endemic to US society. In her post-program interview, Brooklyn commented about how moving and enriching it was to be in community with others who were multiracial and her desire to not lose contact with them. For Brooklyn, the people who participated in the study created a new community that supported her through years of feelings of loneliness. She reflected, "The program was a platform where I could share my story and, again, not feel like I'm the only one that's going through this," she said. Brooklyn's experience also highlighted how important it is to heal together. "It is powerful to know others have gone through similar experiences as me, and when they shared, I was able to reflect on it and move on, and also learned things from them." For Brooklyn, support doesn't just look like affirmation but involves listening to "different perspectives" that she understands to be intertwined with her own life and overall well-being.

Therefore, MCAM's major risk was to be mindful of how to offer next steps of support for the participants of the program after it ended. In particular, new communities that are spacious and nonjudgmental and committed to racial justice (and each of these are qualities needed for BIPOC self-enrichment) should be prioritized.

Blaire left the program with a hope to learn more alongside multiracial others in her community back home as she shared, "I love learning. And I want to . . . read more books . . . because, although I am mixed, I am one individual with a unique experience and perspective of being mixed, but if I can listen to other people who have other perspectives and experiences, I will be enriched." For Blaire, MCAM helped her realize the diversity of multi/racial experience(s). "I can't just live off my own experience of mixed-ness," she remarked, recognizing that she needs "to learn and understand other people's [experiences of mixedness] in order to feel . . . more confident or comfortable speaking about race in our society." Healing cannot come through only one lens or one perspective, and Blaire's post-program interview responses illuminate both the risk of losing support after the program and the program's potential to activate a passion for racial justice in others, even if they had no prior exposure to conversations about multi/racial experience(s) and monoracism. "I think my big takeaway is like, I want to learn more. I want to be in community and hear more stories," Blaire concluded.

Continuing on in intimate community (beyond the initial experience of practicing MCAM) cannot be assumed in the highly individualized, racially traumatizing, and multiracial experience-denying patterns common to North America. To respond to this risk, it is vital for MCAM to help participants identify what resources in their life might be available to further a sense of loving community within which they can reflect on their own multiraciality. MCAM can help them identify community in numerous ways, but I offer five from my own experiences here: nature-based practices of communion with the cosmos that foster listening to the earth as one who speaks; intrapersonal resources such as Internal Family Systems; interpersonal relationships such as with psychologists or spiritual directors; institutional relationships such as with religious (or other common ground) groups committed to racial justice, such as the Society of Critical Mixed-Race Studies; as well as communities that follow contemplative and socially conscious practices such as the Association of Contemplative Mind in Higher Education.

Affirmations of MCAM

While there were risks that became clear throughout the program, there were also key affirmations that provided evidence as to how the program's unique approach empowered multiracial people in tending to their own racialized experiences through spirituality. Five affirmations that came from my qualitative research were: a movement from race avoidance to race consciousness, a movement from self-judgment to self-acceptance, an increased awareness of the interdependencies of Life, a newfound desire toward reconciliation with differences through processes of interiority, and the significance of open and emergent spiritualities.

Through participation in MCAM, the participants increased their consciousness of race and experiences of racialization. Blaire's group reflection showcases how MCAM helped her to learn about racialization in the United States, particularly how it affects multiracial people. The concept of "micro-differential racialization" was particularly important for Blaire's reflection. She said,

> I had never really thought about how [micro-differential racialization] happens and had to think about how this is different from code-switching, which I definitely do depending on who I am with. But [micro-differential racialization] is more of others putting me in whatever box is most convenient for them at the time, and I have definitely had small experiences of this, especially with white friends who may think it's okay to say something negative about Mexicans and think it won't upset me because it "doesn't apply to me because I'm basically white."

Blaire recognized that such acts of colorism may benefit her in a white supremacist society, but "it perpetuates really negative ideas about others who are darker than I am." Finding resonance with the story of Gloria Anzaldúa, Blaire expressed an empowering comfort as she realized that there are transformative ways to engage race and racism as a mixed-race person. Even amid rising feelings of anger and frustration, "I thought the way in which [Anzaldúa] sees the multiracial experience was beautiful, and I want to see it more like that," Blaire said.

Molly also recognized that race shows up differently based on context. As such, engagement must be adaptive rather than prescribed or avoided. For Molly, meditation became necessary so that she could "have energy and . . . be filled with compassion and come out of a place of overflow [with] more mental capacity to engage racial situations." The program's engagement with CMRS helped shape the contexts of meditation, too, and Molly said that this engagement showed "that there is historical and sociological backing to a lot of these ideas that we were talking about." For Will, MCAM led him to understand broader contexts of race and how it works in society, particularly how it has impacted mixed-race people. He lifted up "having all of the different types of negative racial tactics used on multiracial people laid out" as an experience that allowed him "to pinpoint certain painful parts" in his own life when he has been complicit with it, "even taken part in it without truly knowing."

Other participants grew toward racial consciousness through identifying thoughts and/or emotions that came along with racialized experiences. Faye shared in her pre-program interview that she never likes to talk about race with others because it is too loaded. In her post-program interview, she shared, "I definitely think that this program made me realize that race is something that should be talked about more than it is." Faye was able to give voice to her emotions and feelings regarding race—such as pain and anger—for the first time as she recognized that "probably a lot of people that feel the same way as me, and maybe even more so, that just aren't being heard." The importance of having a group that has similar racialized experiences was clearly important for Faye. "The most impactful thing for me about this was really knowing that there's other people my age that have similar experiences, because, obviously, I never really talked to anyone about it, because I never really had friends that I could talk to about it with," Faye said. "So that was cool, to hear at least." It was clear that a major success of the program was moving participants past a colorblind approach to a more race-conscious approach.

The second affirmation of MCAM that emerged through the study was an extension of self-acceptance. The participants each expressed an increased capacity to heal from self-judgment toward their multidimensional and racialized experiences. Faye expressed a newfound desire to begin to identify her needs and tend to her own emotions herself.

> I feel like I need to be more intentional to be in tune with my spirit and my emotions and allow myself to reflect on how I feel and even when it's hard to feel negative emotions. Taking the U-turn is not easy for me. I think it's hard for me to stop myself when emotions feel heavy. It's hard for me to pause and show myself compassion in those moments, and, even after those moments are subsided, I still feel shameful that I let myself feel that way. Self-compassion means to let go of any other negative emotions and to love myself no matter what happens or what circumstance I find myself in. Self-compassion means to me as a multiracial person to understand that it is okay to not have everything figured out, and it is okay to be confused about my identity, but to love myself anyways. This practice helps my ability to have more compassion for myself for sure. It's a great reminder to do so and to remember

> this in times I get overwhelmed with anxiety or depression that there's a better way to view myself and to love myself with compassion.

Faye's experience demonstrates how MCAM helped nourish her spiritual and overall well-being as she was able to finish the program with this profound insight: "I now see that I don't just identify with one race, but two. . . . I wouldn't say I'm fully one or fully other, but I'm just both at the same time equally" is a radical statement of self-acceptance and resistance. Other participants, such as Will, shared how self-compassion in racialized moments can produce self-love and acceptance. In the final session, he said publicly to the group, "I love being multiracial because I am a product and proof that I do not have to be categorized."

Sean noted, "I enjoyed this program and how it brought some light to how I can operate better on treating myself. I focus so much on practicing compassion to others that I can forget to show myself compassion." He recalled that before participating in MCAM, he would completely identify as Hispanic "because the only other option was Black, white, Hispanic, or other." But through MCAM, Sean moved toward integration, creating a newfound desire to reclaim his Indian heritage. He then shared, "For a long time, I had barely scratched the surface of my roots in India, and now I really would like to go there and understand these roots."

For Will, MCAM cultivated a space for him to create his own definition of what being multiracial means to him, rather than trying to fit into any one prescribed racial group definition. "As a half-Black, half-white male," Will said, "I am always confronted with different ways I 'should act' or certain music I 'should listen to' or even certain ways I 'should talk.' It makes me really angry to be honest, and I do not appreciate the ways either of my ethnicities have been stereotyped to act, speak, and just be." MCAM affirms that there is power in self-acceptance and knowing one's deepest identity as able to affirm all aspects of one's experience.

Ellie shared that this program helped her become more aware of her thought-life, including biases and stereotypes that she holds against others and how to be more compassionate within herself to live differently. MCAM "helps me internally to catch myself in thoughts and think 'I am going to think these things' [or] 'it is human to think these things.' And I don't say 'it's human' to make an excuse for it," she stated, "but . . . people have thoughts and it pops into your head. So, now [that the thought is there] to focus on it and catch myself and say 'No. That is not true.'" The internal process that Ellie described helped her notice how her thoughts "fit into a stereotype" that may be rooted in distant experiences and dehumanize the person who triggered the thought. This admission from Ellie was a humble and honest recognition of growth in her ability to attend to her thought-life through this program, which can empower her to now change how she interacts with diverse others.

And finally, Brooklyn reflected on increased capacities as a woman who is racialized Black to embrace her full self as multiracial. "Growing up multiracial was not always easy. Depending on the group I was with, I remember there were times in middle and high school where I felt like I was not being 'Black enough' or 'white enough,'" she said. It was difficult for Brooklyn to accept herself from a young age because others would not accept her. "Even during my freshman year of college," she recalled, "someone I had grown very close to called me 'white-washed.'" As with Ellie, the racialization that Brooklyn experienced was certainly influenced by broader societal forces. For Brooklyn, the force of monoracist categorization was particularly strong.

She reflected that along with others, she was "trying to fit myself into one box, when, in reality, I'm a combination of multiple boxes . . . a unique combination." MCAM became an experience of rejuvenation for her as she claims her full experience and resists how others may racialize her. "Through the practices this week," she said, "I was reminded that I need to show myself grace and understanding just as much as I show others. I come from a mixed family, and I am still learning to fully appreciate and connect with both sides, and that is okay." Brooklyn's and Ellie's stories both illuminate how multiracial people, particularly those with dark skin, are excluded from monoracial backgrounds and groups. Even more, these reflections show how this program helped participants to confront the internalized oppression within themselves and engage race compassionately.

The third affirmation I discovered in MCAM was the transformational awareness participants encountered through paying attention to the interdependencies that characterize the cosmos. Ellie shared her newfound understanding of how her life is constituted by interdependence that supports her every moment and has implications for the ways she moves and acts in the world. "I would definitely say this experience has helped me to understand what is going on within myself. Like, literally the world is your whole life," she observed, "so, [I come] with more awareness now to the ripple effect that I make for the world to be a gentler place." Rather than reducing her experience to that of only one life, Ellie now sees that every action she takes personally is important to all of life. Being aware both of how rough the world can be and how we are all interconnected, Ellie began to ask, "Okay, well, how can I make it a nicer world for myself? How can I make it a nicer world for those around me?" This expansive interconnection, she said, "is empowering."

The interdependent connections were also moving for Sean

as they led him to be more open with diverse religious others by finding connections and similarities. He realized that, through the practice and power of compassionate spirituality, he can enter dialogue with those whom previously he may have judged or kept his distance from. MCAM, he said, "is great for people of all different backgrounds, no matter if you're just spiritual, or if you're different backgrounds of faith [because] it literally allows you to see similarities between" groups whose societies often separate. This program also expanded the way his spirituality is communal, so he can be a better listener who is open and empathetic regarding what others share.

The interdependencies were not just reducible to sharing connection with other humans but also were discovered through the guided meditation practices that allowed the participants to become aware of themselves as embodied and cosmic beings. This was especially significant as those who have experienced racial oppression are not just emotionally or psychologically wounded but also physically wounded through exploitation, abuse, and imprisonment. Blaire recognized that "even in that moment of racialized difference when I felt disconnected from other people, I was always connected to the earth and the foundational principle of inherently sacred compassion." MCAM helped participants to restore connections to the wisdom of physicality and embodiment. Blaire connected sacred compassion with the wisdom of embodiment.

> Sacred compassion, for me, meant that, to some degree, I will always be taken care of and loved without having to do anything; that simply being alive shows that I am taken care of by the earth. As I recognize that, I am able to return that favor to the earth. I spent a lot of time feeling very connected to the earth in the sense that I am receiving compassion from the air I breathe

> and then returning and giving that back to the earth as I exhale. As I am still figuring out what my spirituality looks like, having this sense of connectedness to the divinity of nature was incredibly spiritual and helpful for me.

In Blaire's reflection, she makes an important observation for MCAM by pointing out the spiritual reality of abundance that permeates her every moment. Embracing embodiment as a cosmic being is a lasting knowing that she can return to even amid the difficulties and chaos of life. She shared how this program has helped her to see how she is a recipient of the earth's sacred compassion. Through her experiences in MCAM, she is better connected to her embodied reality and encouraged to embrace her physicality as essential to her spiritual life.

For Will, recognizing interdependency entailed noticing that the sacred was all around him in the here and now, giving him the power to live in and from peace, despite the reality of broken human relations. Like Blaire, Will connected sacred compassion and embodied connection. He said, "Life is always giving you something compassionate. This is demonstrated by the ground we stand on and the air we breathe." With his regular practice, Will became aware of the ways that the more-than-human world influenced his spiritual experiences. He expressed a humility toward human relationships with the cosmos, noting, "If no compassion is ever shown to us by another human, I believe God's beautifully constructed world has the ability to bring us peace and compassion through nature." Each of these reflections depicts various ways that spiritual experiences can ground multiracial people's experiences of interdependent support for their own life within the cosmos. They also reveal important connections between present experiences of mysterious interrelatedness and memories of connection that live within our embodied multiplicity.

The fourth affirmation is that taking a spiritual approach to multiraciality fostered an increased desire within participants to reconcile differences by way of their own interiority. Ellie offered a particularly powerful example. Learning about racial oppression in the United States was more difficult than she anticipated. "The program helped to expose my thoughts and actions . . . [but] not necessarily to look back on the past and feel bad," she noticed. MCAM's spiritual framing allowed her to feel revitalized and empowered to confront oppressive moments or systems through the power of connection. Ellie continued, "It was like, 'shit happens,' but you can take steps now to move forward and do things to make life better. I think that is so important in relationships and these conversations, being aware of your shortcomings and [yet] not to dwell on [the shortcomings]." Rather than judging or offering immediate advice, MCAM helped her to begin to pause and just listen to herself and others more deeply. "A major takeaway for me," she said, "was the amount of times I have tried to get someone to see the 'brighter side' of things versus just sitting with them in their grief." The "sitting with others" that she describes is one way to understand how efforts of reconciliation can be improved through deep interiority.

Brooklyn was also galvanized through MCAM to think about new ways she can invite and be a resource to others in the sacred work of racial justice. "I know that it can feel like walking on eggshells when entering into a conversation about race, but that does not mean we should avoid it," she stated. With her experiences in MCAM as her base, Brooklyn's goal is to develop true relationships that overcome the disconnection she has experienced before while circumstances worsen. She used language of courageous embrace, writing, "I think we should embrace the conversation about race; avoiding this topic will only make things worse and possibly cause more tension. I am invited to engage race in the future through a lens of respect and courage." She recognized, though, that the important work to do cannot come at the cost of her own emotional well-being. The courageous embrace must be rooted in "the spiritual practice of extending compassion to others," including to the self. With respect and courage, Brooklyn feels equipped "to create spaces where my friends and family can feel comfortable sharing their stories and opinions." The practices of MCAM revealed opportunities for compassion that are rooted in the self's interiority and facilitate deeper relationships with others.

Blaire found that this practice invites her into a freedom to respond to others in ways that both transcend her assumptions and make attempts at healing race relations with creative compassion. "Creative compassion," she said, "includes being more of an active listener and being willing to ask people questions to get to the root of their words and actions so that I can better understand where they are coming from." In her case, this means to educate when necessary "but also respecting [her] experience enough to protect it when necessary" for her own self-care.

Finally, three participants emphasized how the program offered inspiration in new reconciliatory acts amid the world's suffering. They described MCAM as helping them realize their own spiritual power and strength rather than fear or hostility. Will remarked, "Our ability to respond is amazing. It is really cool to me that no matter what situation we are presented with we have complete control of our response and how that can make a difference in the world." For Molly, we cannot pretend about the realities of racism and our capacity for constructive response, but we also cannot act like we are impotent. "Unfortunately," she said, "we do not have control over the different forms of racism/colorism that people display, but we do have control over how we respond to it." Rather than waiting for someone else to make a change, participants have decided to become the change they seek, reconciling differences in the world in themselves.

Beginning within, Will realized "that when [anger that boils within me] is brought up, my ability to listen disappears because I only want the other person to understand my view of this situation." Molly's observation about controlling our response is particularly important in situations like Will's. She also admitted, "It is a very difficult thing to grasp and implement because people can be hurtful, but it is also very empowering" to realize one's own power within. Will connected the power within to sacred compassion in relationships with others, writing, "Maybe, if I have sacred compassion and confidence in my skin and abilities, then I can talk with more meaning." For both Molly and Will, approaching the world through compassion is not a weak idealism. Will framed it this way:

> This gives us so much power to live our lives in a positive and meaningful manner while also taking power away from nasty comments or negativity. After this program, I came to a cool conclusion about myself. I picked the experience of being called too white or not Black enough. I chose to feel those feelings and relive that experience over again to see what I could learn about myself and that memory. I realized that usually anger boils up in me and I can snap back at the person in extreme ways, or take a small comment too far when it is said to me. . . . This exercise showed me that maybe if I ask questions and listen very intentionally to the

> speaker then I can get somewhere with myself and the conversation. . . . I was very happy to go through this exercise and will be using it again to sharpen this skill of visualization. Thank you so much! This has really been helping me work through certain things and sharpen myself.

The third participant who shared these sentiments was Sean. In his post-program interview, he shared an anecdote about how MCAM has helped him in his daily life even after such a short practice. During and after this program, Sean built up resources of compassion that enabled him to humanize another person and find a way toward connection and healing rather than isolation and separation.

> Yesterday I was going to a gas station and this person honked at me for no reason and it was like rush hour traffic. I was already edgy and I got out of the car and I ended up staring at this person. We ended up staring and she just kind of just gave me like a "what?" And I wanted to say something back and instead I gave her a smile and I gave her a peace sign and I wanted to challenge myself. I was like, I felt this voice in me, go up to her and go pay for her gas right now. And I was like, no, don't, and I had this other voice, like, don't do that. Are you kidding me? She just insulted you. Why would you do that? And this is coming from a broke college student. I'm like, I have no money. I'm like, okay. I'm like, and I feel like I should have at least given her $10 to pay for some of her gas. I really wanted to. So that's, I think, how sacred compassion definitely affected me and seeing situations like that, especially when I'm predisposed

> to a reaction out of anger, that reaction and turning it into an act of kindness.

Each of these testimonies bears witness to the reconciling potency of a spiritual approach to multiraciality that weaves spirituality and critical mixed-race theory. MCAM is not simply theoretical. As a spiritual practice, it contributes to the everyday lives of participants and those with whom they come into contact in meaningful and tangible ways.

A final affirmation received through MCAM was the significance and importance of open and emergent spiritualities to undergird anti-racist efforts. Especially for the growing mixed-race population who inherit multiple cultural and/or religious traditions from their families of origin and are coming of age in an increasingly globalized and pluralistic world, anti-racist activism, movements, and organizations must foster spiritual depth and multiplicity as core to their efforts. MCAM helped root participants in a spiritual practice while also encouraging the notion that spirituality can be renewed and re-created person to person and community to community. A both/and orientation to spirituality helped many participants to move beyond fundamentalist expressions of spirituality and religion that they were handed through racist institutions, and it helped them reframe activist assumptions about spirituality and religion being disengaged from the real world or struggle.

While only a few participants came into the program with a prior commitment to a specific religious tradition, all were very open to exploring how spirituality could be adapted for them as a mixed-race person. Ellie described MCAM as "an awesome setup [with] meditations as smooth as they could go . . . almost like a podcast meditation." The exploration of spirituality does not need to try and convert someone. Rather, Blaire experienced MCAM asking her to be open to the uniqueness of her own spirituality and also to integrate aspects from her past that had been difficult for her. She noticed the presence of some familiar "Christian traditional readings" but also said, "I think the way that these practices were done, I didn't necessarily feel connected to a deity. I feel like I more so felt very connected to myself." MCAM demonstrated that movements cannot adequately attend to the well-being of mixed-race people without compassionately exploring the depth dimension of spiritual experiences. "I think we started with great and intriguing questions [that] set it up in a great opening way to explore spirituality," Ellie said. In that exploration, one will discover that multi/racial experience(s) of spirituality contribute in important and particular ways to healing from racism and colonization in North America.

Because multiracial people recognize that and how their racial status disrupts prescribed processes of racialization, exploring spiritualities within anti-racist spaces may give multiracial people a unique chance to share how processes of reconciliation can occur from their own experiences of reconciliation within themselves. When multi/racial experience(s) are taken seriously in these spaces, mixed-race people may even be some of the forerunners who create and imagine new and emergent spiritualities that can more adequately address the multiple crises through which we are currently living. The return to mysticism and spirituality is greatly beneficial for multiracial people and enables us to hold our multiplicity and be open to the spontaneity of Life as it disrupts other preconceived and oppressively imposed categories of separation.

Future Possibilities of Transforming MCAM

As I mentioned earlier, this study was designed with attention to change and the ability to grow. In addition to the risks and affirmations that have already been discussed, I am compelled to offer a few concrete changes that could be made to MCAM to make it more effective for people to engage in the future. These suggestions arise from practicing with the participants and from studying their interview data. First, race avoidance or race denial as a common starting place should be normalized. Second, intersectionality should be highlighted as the through-line for building bonds of multiraciality. Third, each of the sessions should creatively utilize emergent technologies that can allow for spiritual connections to be established and deepened.

First, MCAM facilitators should begin the program with an assumption that most of the participants will not have had experiences of spiritually supportive communities that nurtured their unique multi/racial experience(s). For many multiracial people, many barriers exist to engaging the realities of race and racism. Though such a statement may seem simple on its face, it is a profound realization that textures the experiences that participants bring with them into the program. The first barrier is the awareness that most multiracial people will come into the program with repeated experiences of racial trauma. This trauma happens in a few ways. One way is because many have parents who have had different racial experiences from them. Therefore, the parents do not know how to connect to the mixed-race experiences of their children. Second, many parents themselves have had different racialized experiences from each other, and they have likely not found empowered ways of relating to this fact with each other and with their children. Additionally, because multiracial people are a relatively new and emerging population within the United States, it is not common for multiracial people to have met many others who share their experience of being mixed other than siblings, if they have siblings at all. The lack of social connection with other multiracial people results in patterns of race avoidance or denial that are only exacerbated when mixed-race people enter racial justice spaces as young adults to discover systemic and structural monoracial bias, rendering their multiraciality invisible again. To address this history, I recommend that MCAM facilitators start with an assumption that, while many multiracial people might be aware of race and racism at a social or political level, very few participants will have had access to any spiritually supportive spaces that have nurtured them within their capacities to compassionately tend to their unique racialized experiences as multiracial people.

Second, building bonds of multiraciality can be greatly enhanced through a nuanced approach that embraces intersectionality. While the program was able to help participants understand how multiraciality causes them to be racialized differently from setting to setting, participants mentioned how they would have benefitted even more by reflecting on their experiences of marginalization through lenses such as gender, socioeconomic status, dis/ability, or language. While I still believe the space should begin with an emphasis on race, more time can be taken to develop an approach that validates the social identity that participants perceive to be most visible in first encounters with others, and, more specifically, how this could greatly change moment to moment and context to context. Molly poignantly discussed this with the group about midway through the program. "Since I have a disability," she said, "I think that is different for the racial piece because [race] is not only the first thing people see." Disability impacts the way that Molly is racialized. She continued, "With something like gender, I think it just feeds into all of it depending on where I am. Then socioeconomic status feeds into my experience, too."

Intersectional analysis would have impacted each participant differently, helping them further locate their experiences of racialization. Ellie comes from a Spanish-speaking home and reflected on how language, perceived socioeconomic status, and educational background all impact how she is racialized. "Spanish," she said, "is looked at as a negative thing in our society, and people who speak it [Spanish] first are looked at as dumb or even poor because of it." Furthermore, Ellie pointed out that the actual ability to speak Spanish (or a second "poor" language) might be assumed because of the racializing process. "Most of us [who speak Spanish] know English as our first language and aren't fluent in anything else, yet we are treated worse if others think we are bilingual," she said. While many participants found Gloria Anzaldúa's example of intersectionality helpful when it comes to thinking about the ways various aspects of social identity arise in the matrix of oppression, participants still struggled to connect the multidimensionality of their own multiracial experiences to one another. Without their own intersectional analysis, participants, therefore, remained more individualistic in expression. More time should be devoted to reflecting on how various oppressions occur in initial encounters so that participants may be able to more clearly see the fluid natures of what liberation may look and feel like.

By consciously incorporating and centering intersectionality in the guided meditations, future programming would be able to foster a greater awareness of oppression in the participants' own experiences and be able to build a better foundation for how they engage their experiences as they are intertwined. With a greater focus on intersectionality, this will make plain the many ways that racism manifests itself and can also begin to help participants make connections in struggles for justice with people who are not multiracial. Realizing intersectionality as a core part of the program could allow for more intersectional coalitions and partnerships with other groups to emerge as the participants move on from the practice.

Third, it is important to tend to the ways that spiritual presence can be fostered virtually. One of the most important qualities of the program was the support that participants "felt." While the shift in group dynamics after engaging in spiritual practice together at the end of each session was noticeable, spiritual practice is the foundation of the program. The whole experience could be improved by choosing to also begin each session with spiritual practice. Facilitators should also make additional considerations of facial cues and nonverbal communication in the practice because it is easy to miss a lot of these interpersonal dynamics when facilitating a program online.

While one of the greatest strengths of the program was the fact that participants could experience it from any location and at their own pace, the program could benefit from more thought on how digital technology could be used to invite presence and attention to oneself and one another. Opening and closing spiritual practices could help invite and set expectations for presence. While a few participants shared that they felt the program would have benefitted from more personal check-ins, I think this longing for deeper connection could come through shared awareness practices where we focus attentively on more fully embracing the reality of others in the space. In future iterations of this program, I want to offer more attuned spaces that allow for the deepening of personal and collective spirituality and incorporate new technologies like virtual reality in ways that support Life as a whole.

Conclusion

In this chapter, I have detailed a new spiritual program called Mysticism, Compassion, and Multiraciality, which intends to support mixed-race people in the awareness of their unique experience as a Multiracial Christophany. Featuring the participants' insights, my qualitative evaluation of the data demonstrated a core feature of MCAM, centering multi/racial experience(s) in spiritual formation, healing, and well-being. The evaluations were structured to address risks, affirmations, and possibilities for future iterations of the program. I discussed risks that became clear when attempting to host this program online as well as when working with people who have little or no background information about race theories and some or no affiliation with institutional religion. I shared affirmations of the program, including the need and desire for more spaces to be created that engage conversations on race and racism from mixed-race perspectives and in ways that are embedded within commitments to spirituality and collectivist approaches to social change. I concluded with practical possibilities for improving the experience in the future that not only will enhance the program but also may inspire others to create spaces such as these for others to tend to the impacts of race, racism, and racial oppression. This book frames both the practice and evaluation of MCAM within Panikkar's commitment to mysticism and intercultural dialogue for the purpose of genuine world transformation. Overcoming internalized oppression is a foundational starting place that can enable free and creative actions to be imagined that can, in turn, heal the violence of the world in a spirit of companionship and solidarity, one compassionate movement at a time.

4

Discerning New Paths of Multiraciality: A Call to New Worlds

Discerning new action is at once a risk and a movement of joy. Through the process of embracing our contingency as human beings, we somehow mysteriously come across the truth that our value as human beings is not made up of the outcome of our efforts but simply is. This mystical realization is not reserved for a few "holy people" with mountaintop experiences. It is realized when a person knows who they ultimately are and, in this knowing, lives out this awareness co-participating with the adventurous mystery of Life. This program (MCAM) invites all to consider who we truly are, and from that knowing, how our lives and actions should change. What are the new ways we are being invited to live? Perhaps virtuous service to ourselves and neighbors? Or loving presence in the midst of difficulty? A deeper invitation to solidarity with suffering? My hope is that may we all be inspired by the resilience of Life, the courage that comes from knowing we are loved, and the importance of slowing down so that we might touch the hurting places with divine tenderness and mercy.—*Aizaiah Yong,* journal entry, Los Angeles, CA, 2019

Creating New Worlds through Multiracial Cosmotheandrism: A Practical Theology of Multiraciality in Nine Sutra

In this final chapter, I weave together the insights gathered from the previous chapters to present Multiracial Cosmotheandrism, a practical theology for multiraciality. The practical theological proposal of this book emerged through a triadic contemplative dialogue between the lived experiences and spiritualities of mixed-race people (who occupy life at the intersections of racial, ethnic, religious, and cultural traditions), the cosmotheandric life of Raimon Panikkar, and the qualitative findings from a newly fashioned spiritual formation program (MCAM). This practical theology pays homage to Raimon Panikkar and is my personal response to his call for "replanting," both embracing the past as well as creatively transforming it in the present.[1]

In Panikkar's remembrance, this final chapter follows his well-known *sutra* style.[2] My proposal for a practical theology of multi/racial experience(s), then, is not a set of "theses to be defended . . . rather, condensations of experiences lived." Such a style entails that "it is up to the reader to make a carpet out of them, perhaps even a tapestry" with the insights as

1. Raimon Panikkar, *Mysticism and Spirituality, Part Two: Spirituality, the Way of Life*, ed. Milena Carrara Pavan (Maryknoll, NY: Orbis Books, 2014), 228.

2. There are numerous sutra that one may find when studying Panikkar's work, a few of those that have most impacted me are "Nine Sutra on Christophany," in *Christianity, Part Two: A Christophany*, ed. Milena Carrara Pavan (Maryknoll, NY: Orbis Books, 2015), 244–47, "Nine Sutra on Peace," in *Cultures and Religions in Dialogue, Part One: Pluralism and Interculturality*, ed. Milena Carrara Pavan (Maryknoll, NY: Orbis Books, 2018), 205–12, and "Aspects of a Cosmotheandric Spirituality," in *Trinitarian and Cosmotheandric Vision*, ed. Milena Carrara Pavan (Maryknoll, NY: Orbis Books, 2021), 191–222.

"threads linking us to the past and opening us to the future."[3] I see my practical theology of multiraciality in alignment with what Scott Eastham believed may have been Panikkar's deepest hope for his dialogue partners, namely, to "turn and return to deepen their own traditions with fresh eyes and transformative energies."[4] As a practical theologian who is also multiracial, I call for the dismantling of all forms of oppression in the world and the ongoing creation of emergent spiritualities that will be the driving forces through which new worlds of harmony can be realized. I offer nine sutra as ways of inviting others to ways of being and knowing that embrace more fully the "experience of life as part of the cosmic adventure,"[5] starting with those who are multiracial. The nine sutra of Multiracial Cosmotheandrism speak to the interwoven disciplines that are foundational to this book: mysticism and spirituality, critical mixed-race studies, and practical theology. (1) *Be Practical,* (2) *Do Theology,* (3) *Embrace Multiraciality,* (4) *Live Inspired*, (5) *Love Life,* (6) *Reflect Philosophy,* (7) *Accept the "And,"* (8) *Make Way for Mysticism,* and (9) *Remember Raimon Panikkar.*

Be Practical

Panikkar turns the pithy reminder that we are called human *be-ings* not human *doings* into a deeper observation about our connections with one another and Life. He writes, "The major stumbling block to a spontaneous outflowing of the experience

3. Panikkar also saw sutra as "neither totally Western or Eastern" but a fecundation of diverse ways of knowing and being and which require that a certain level of consciousness be attained to understand them. See *Christianity, Part Two*, 243.

4. Scott Eastham, "After Panikkar," in Gerard Hall and Joan Hendriks, eds., *Dreaming a New Earth: Raimon Panikkar and Indigenous Spiritualities* (Preston, Victoria [Australia]: Mosaic Press, 2013), 24–40.

5. "Home Page," Fundació Vivarium Raimon Panikkar, 2022.

of Life within us is our preoccupation with doing, to the detriment of being and living."[6] In contrast to late-stage capitalism's creeds, Life cannot be reduced to what is produced. Nor can life only be the accumulation of goods that separates us from earth and binds us to "free" markets and global capital. If one lives enslaved to a do-list, one becomes an endless set of transactions, and life becomes a world bank. Banks do not know happiness. Life is more than a pile of receipts.

To *be practical* does not mean to avoid the intellect and focus on what we do without the intellect, but to overcome the tendency that we have to get in the way of Life's flow. To *be practical* means to practice living from our Be-ing! In Multiracial Cosmotheandrism, this means that how we relate to a racialized world ought to be informed by our deepest identity, moving beyond labels and categories. This does not mean labels and identifications are unimportant and should be discarded altogether, for they certainly influence each of us and are important factors in discerning how we engage Life. Yet Multiracial Cosmotheandrism recognizes that such markers are not the ultimate source of Life, and, therefore, we will only know what to do practically when we know our deepest identity in relation to Being itself.

When Life is lived from our spiritual and compassionate core, what we have considered to be impossible becomes possible. And as multiracial people, we make the world from our spiritual and compassionate cores and powerfully embody the transformative quality of possibility. Multiracial people embody what has previously been marked as incompatible and beautify the world through their lived presence and creative connec-

6. Raimon Panikkar, *Mysticism and Spirituality, Part One: Mysticism, the Fullness of Life*, ed. Milena Carrara Pavan (Maryknoll, NY: Orbis Books, 2014), xxii.

tions. By bringing together what has been forcibly separated and erased by systems of oppression, new life is offered which no violence can erase. While many groups and cultures of the world remain tribal and ethnocentric, multiracial people can be one type of forerunner that overcomes these isolating tendencies. Multiracial Cosmotheandrism centers the power of relationship building with distant others and imagines new ways of sharing and loving the world through reciprocity and cross-fertilization.

In a time of polarization, misunderstanding, and self-righteous judgment, Multiracial Cosmotheandrism calls for a renewed *practice of being* by harmonizing what seems contradictory or even impossible. This reconciliatory posture paves the way for the renewal and transformation of all. The time is ripe for a new consciousness that overcomes blame, internalized oppression, and scapegoating that encourages becoming a co-participant in the work of (re)creation. Multiracial Cosmotheandrism calls for a plurality of emergent spiritualities and spiritual practices that can lead to many forms of "new consciousness" that synthesize divergent ideas, traditions, cultures, approaches, and wisdoms for the purposes of participating in the healing of life as a whole.

Do Theology

The adage "do not tell me, show me" speaks to the hollowness of words if they are not backed up by one's actions. While Life cannot be fully expressed through words, Life can be deepened and transformed through them. This is especially true for *theology*, for they are words, thoughts, and ideas that gesture toward the Unspeakable and Unknowable. For some, theology is talk about God; for others it speaks of a different symbol or myth. This is important. Yet, no matter how important the particular words are when we write and study, *doing theology* is about the ways our theologies create openings to *live* more fully and more compassionately. There is a great longing in the world for theology to be felt, experienced, and encountered, especially amid suffering. For multiracial people, suffering is psychological, social, and even spiritual. This fact calls for theology to be done in new ways.

New theologies are already beginning to emerge in North America. While many younger people increasingly identify as nonreligious, signaling the widespread skepticism of religious institutions and decrease in formal theological study, in some ways there is an increased openness to explore life's "ultimate concerns"[7] anew. A recent study[8] shows how young adults are finding creative ways outside of organized religion to build community, explore meaning, and ritualize experiences of the sacred with others. The study is an example of how theology itself remains essential even while its methods, findings, or even religious institutions change. Multiracial Cosmotheandrism is one new and important theology that calls for life to be more fully incarnated by tending to one's racialized suffering with tenderness and mercy. However, any theology must be careful that it does not hide behind the eloquence of words without paying attention to how it creates a fuller embodiment that matches.

While Multiracial Cosmotheandrism is a new theology, it also embraces impermanence. The words used to describe it are not intended to be read as final but as invitational. Though I have taken caution when choosing words in my writing, all words are incomplete in some way; or, perhaps, it may be accurate to say that all words usher in a new completion of the world

7. Paul Tillich, *Dynamics of Faith* (New York: Harper & Row, 1957), 14.

8. Tom Layman reports on one such study done by Angie Thurston and Casper ter Kuile in his article "CrossFit as Church? Examining How We Gather," *Harvard Divinity School News Archive* (November 4, 2015).

they try to grasp! Words become powerful to the degree that they become transparent to the Reality that precedes them. The theological task of Multiracial Cosmotheandrism is, then, to encourage people to open themselves to the Spirit that is alive and at work in and through them so that Life may flow more freely. Doing theology with Multiracial Cosmotheandrism means that we pave the way for (and are willing to accept) life in its newest and most unexpected forms. For some, this book may allow for a greater awareness of the sacred reality that is at work in the depth dimension of experiences of multiraciality. And it may not do this for others, but embracing impermanence resists speaking definitively and exhaustively. If the book is successful in its theological task, then perhaps other multiracial people will find something that resonates deep within them, compelling them to do theology in a way that has yet to be uttered.

Embrace Multiraciality

One cannot adequately understand the present context of North America without understanding the histories of colonization, racism, and racial oppression. The empire known as the United States of America was founded and expanded through the intentional enslavement of nonwhite people and religious justifications for this racist system. The empire known as Canada has been forced to reckon with the legacy of "Christian" boarding schools for the Aboriginal peoples who are First Nations, Inuit, and Métis peoples as burial sites of murdered people have been discovered in numerous waves.[9] However, race and racial oppression do not only affect nonwhites, but all of life because of the ways that white supremacy presupposes, enforces, and legit-

9. Ian Austen, "How Thousands of Indigenous Children Vanished in Canada," *New York Times*, June 7, 2021.

imizes hierarchies of separateness and injustice. Multiraciality disrupts unjust hierarchical patterns by disturbing essentialist notions of identity and demands mutuality and love to be at the core of all relations.

Multiracial Cosmotheandrism argues that Life is found in many forms and that each form is multidimensional and polyvocal. Therefore, no one form, culture, language, tradition, experience, or image should be engaged through the hierarchical flattening of Life to only one dimension. A multidimensional and intersectional approach is needed. Multiracial Cosmotheandrism acknowledges the mystery of multidimensionality and calls us to embrace multiraciality, problematizing universal definitions and hierarchical structures that perpetuate domination. Multiracial Cosmotheandrism is rooted in the awareness of the vast diversity and plurality of reality and demands for practices of hospitality that cultivate genuine friendship. True hospitality can be realized only when capacities of honor, compassion, and nonjudgmental presence have been developed. The time is ripe for us to learn afresh these skills and to respect the particularities of diverse experiences that weave within oneself, the experiences of another person, and other-than-human Life. Multiracial Cosmotheandrism asks that we avoid reductionism, allowing for complexity to enrich our bonds of connection, and contends that, in our uniqueness, we each have a role to play that cannot be underestimated. With patience toward the nuanced complexities of Life, Multiracial Cosmotheandrism invites us to deepen our experiences and reconcile polarities within the inner dimensions of our Being through a spirit of trust and solidarity. Multiracial Cosmotheandrism is not aimed at creating one shared experience, but at creating spaciousness within ourselves so that diversity of experiences can be embraced and related to in love.

Live Inspired

The word in-spire can be understood as being breathed into, or being in-breathed. As many cultural and religious traditions acknowledge, breath is the primordial and energetic force that enables all of Life to exist and flourish. Life is made possible through Life's own gift (and exchange) of breath. Life is a flow of generosity that involves all sentient beings. "Nature is our teacher," as Ghanaian eco-spiritual teacher Brother Ishmael Tetteh reminds us.[10] Following Brother Tetteh, Multiracial Cosmotheandrism approaches human experience with a contemplative inclusivity beyond our own species. When contemplating nature's ways, we find that whatever newness arises in Life was made possible only through a previous iteration of another in Life. Multiracial Cosmotheandrism recognizes that life is a gift granted by sheer grace and ought to be cherished, celebrated, and enjoyed. Abundance becomes our norm and known reality. Do we have the capacities to perceive this? In gratitude, we are able to recognize Life brimming over with goodness, beauty, and love. Through the reciprocity of Life, all are sustained, renewed, and re-made.

Inspiration for this book came from abundant gifts of practical theology, critical mixed-race studies, the Cosmotheandric Vision of Raimon Panikkar, the gifts of nature's elements, and the lived experiences of those who participated in the program. The writing of this book is simply a culminating celebration of the gifts received and intended to be given back for the world's flourishing. Multiraciality affirms that one can and must be breathed into from multiple directions for their own life to flourish. Multiraciality warns each of us of the dangerous limi-

10. Ishmael Tetteh, "Nature as a Teacher with Brother Ishmael Tetteh," episode of *Life Conversations* with Life Coach Ade, Blog Talk Radio, 2012.

tations when bias and prejudice favor certain gifts at the degradation of others. The call of Multiracial Cosmotheandrism is to receive a fresh and multidirectional breath from the greatness of Life and to allow joy to be restored. In a world that has been given to despair, anxiety, and hopelessness, a life of joy may be the best inspiration there is.

Love Life

One cannot live fully while excluding any aspect of life. As the great mystic and spiritual teacher Richard Rohr proclaims, "Everything belongs."[11] While media and popular culture tempt us to fixate on certain aspects of life over others, we must learn how to *love* the whole of life if we are to experience freedom. Loving the whole of life is what makes one whole. To love the *whole* of life, we must move to the edges, working to uplift and include those who are oppressed and marginalized. Panikkar called for a church council to be opened "whose concerns would no longer be interecclesial—but would center on far more essential problems. Three quarters of the world's populations live under inhuman conditions. . . . The church cannot be a stranger to such distress, to such institutionalized justice. It cannot remain deaf to the cries of the people, especially of the humble and the poor."[12] In my work with multiracial people, I have noticed a sensitivity in learning to love that which has been rejected by the dominant. Due to the unique and consistent ways in which multiracial people are marginalized from the groups and spaces they find themselves in, not fully fitting in

11. Richard Rohr, *Everything Belongs: The Gift of Contemplative Prayer* (New York: Crossroad Publishing, 1999).

12. Raimon Panikkar, "Eruption of Truth: An Interview with Raimon Panikkar—Religion Online," originally published in *Christian Century*, August 16–23, 2000, 834–36.

prescribed social conventions, they are often keen to notice and emphasize details and nuances that others may easily miss. Multiracial Cosmotheandrism asks for sensitivity to subtlety, to the small things that go overlooked as the only way we can love life holistically. When one is attuned to that which is easily minimized or dismissed by the dominant, transformative capacities to engage Life anew potentialize. From a mystical perspective, the divinity of life is often found through loving what is overlooked. Thérèse of Lisieux, who referred to herself as "the Little Flower of Jesus," is an example of how transformation comes not by the greatness of the act but by the enormity of love that animates even the smallest act.

In healing trauma work, we are also called to love the whole of life, with special attention to what has been disregarded. Spiritual teacher Thomas Hübl describes trauma-informed leadership as a practice that seeks to become aware of "missing information" that has yet to be tended to in the stories of individuals, their communities, organizations, and other institutions at large. He discusses at length how slowing down to become aware of these subtleties (and through being present to ourselves and one another) opens up opportunities to touch our trauma with mercy, presence, and compassion, restoring us and cultivating our flourishing.[13] Often, multiracial people are forced to navigate spaces where their particular wisdoms and intuitions are left out and are, thus, "missing" from understanding race, further compounding structures of oppression. Multiracial Cosmotheandrism calls for the reclamation of their unique wisdoms that easily go unnoticed. Multiracial Cosmotheandrism invites a contemplative posture that includes both intention and attention to be extended to one another and especially our experi-

13. Thomas Hübl, *Healing Collective Trauma: A Process for Integrating Our Intergenerational & Cultural Wounds* (Boulder, CO: Sounds True, 2020).

ences of marginalization. In committing to this at individual, interpersonal, communal, and even cosmic levels, important clues about our healing will emerge, leading us to collectively build deeper connections and bonds.

To love life fully means that we bear witness to the preciousness of the seemingly weak or fragile. What others discard or other-ize, Multiracial Cosmotheandrism calls us to know intimately. Multiracial Cosmotheandrism knows that each being within Life is a microcosm of the macrocosm.[14] Nothing can be tossed out, and, when it is received in love, something changes in the Whole. It is only through the giving and receiving of love that the Life of the world can begin to heal and habits of violence in the heart, mind, body, and spirit will be forever changed.

Reflect Philosophy

To become a philosopher, one should become a loving friend to wisdom, or, rather, receive wisdom as one's loving friend. If we are to allow wisdom to be our companion, we must reflect. We must ponder and consider and allow our knowings to percolate, for we are not microwaves or high-speed internet routers. Reflection takes time and attention.

While one can reflect without becoming wise, wisdom comes only through compassionate reflection. Reflection gives us an opportunity to increase awareness to Life at its depth dimension. When the depth dimension is encountered, it can help a person discern how to live winsomely. Wisdom is not found in achieving certain results or strategizing toward particular outcomes, but it is evident when one becomes a reflection of Truth. A wise person is a person in whose presence others are invited to become wise. This is what it means to

14. Gerard Hall, "Raimon Panikkar: The Human Person."

reflect philosophy. For when we live reflecting Truth, peace is received and becomes the basis for one's actions even amid life's frailties and challenges.

Through this study, I was able to notice this phenomenon in the lives and spiritualities of multiracial people; that is, to notice their ability to witness to the possibility of peace, even in the unfinished process of pursuing wholeness. Multiracial Cosmotheandrism speaks to the possibility of wholeness that multiracial people embody in a special way as they still navigate a world that is monoracist and filled with racial oppression that excludes them. Although the population of multiracial people is still growing and monoracial paradigms dominate racial justice work, multiracial people have still found ways to be at peace with their own experiences, sharing its richness with others. In this way, multiracial people bear witness to a wholeness that is possible, not based upon arriving at a certain point or passing through a particular challenge, but as a way of being in the world that accepts life in its unfinished state. A mindset of acceptance is one of simplicity that delights in the nakedness of life as a gift to cherish and enjoy, even as it continues to unfold. Because multiracial people are still vastly misunderstood and underrepresented, Multiracial Cosmotheandrism demonstrates something special about the human experience. For multiracial people, joy and peace are not ultimately dependent on circumstances but on what is found and received through the capacity to welcome what others reject.

This acceptance of Life in its unfinished state is a form of hope and can be of great resource to those who are often left in despair with the lack of progress from their commitments to social justice. The truth and freedom of our lives are not found through the outcome of our efforts, but in the spirit by which we live and the ways in which we relate to Life in all of its imperfections. This echoes Panikkar's emphasis on hope in his Gifford Lectures.

> What our contemporaries most lack is hope. Everybody has faith—in one thing or another. Love, of all sorts, is also present everywhere. We believe in so many ideas and love so many things, but our culture has little hope. Most people drag their feet along without much enthusiasm and need a variety of stimuli to go on living with a certain joy. Existence, for many, has become boring, when not a burden. Here we need to dispel a misunderstanding: hope is not of the future. Hope should not be confused with a certain optimism about the future which only betrays a pessimism about the present. Hope is not the expectation of a bright tomorrow. Hope is of the invisible.[15]

Multiracial Cosmotheandrism asks others in the world to know and live in this invisible quality of hope, to become a reflection of philosophy, touching all of their experiences with tenderness, forgiveness, and mercy.

Accept the "And"

Binary, oppositional thinking is at the core of the colonial, white supremacist imaginary. Advaita offers an opportunity to overcome this form of dualism by emphasizing the harmonizing of endless difference. Multiracial Cosmotheandrism attests to the ways in which mixed-race people operate a-dualistically, refusing to allow themselves to be "half" but fully "both/and."

15. Raimon Panikkar, *The Rhythm of Being: The Unbroken Trinity* (Maryknoll, NY: Orbis Books, 2010), 10.

This inclusive posture to life is needed if we are to overcome monocultural biases on many levels. In my work with multiraciality, it is evident that mixed-race people disrupt dominant monolithic and monoracial patterns. Multiracial Cosmotheandrism challenges universal understandings of what is "pure, holy, or acceptable," and argues that beauty, goodness, and truth cannot be restricted to any one group or way. Multiracial people resist and dismantle claims to "definitive history" and "universal truth" through their very embodiment of Life. Multiracial Cosmotheandrism develops this resistance, recognizing multiplicity in spiritual approaches that allow Life to be remade for justice and love relative to their societal situatedness.

Practical theology has long paid attention to the ways that history is often told in favor of the oppressor, justifying the repeated dismissal of other voices and presences that demand that new histories be told in religious spaces.[16] As Sheryl Kujawa-Holbrook writes, "naming untold stories of our history will help reveal the needs of the present."[17] With Sheryl Kujawa-Holbrook's encouragement, Multiracial Cosmotheandrism knows that paths of healing can arise only through a disruption of the status quo. And Multiracial Cosmotheandrism attempts to do this by centering the histories and experiences of multiracial people, countering the hegemonic tendencies of exclusion and erasure. Although it can seem disruptive, by "accepting the 'and,'" multiracial people can find freedom to accept the rich complexities of their experiences, which in turn creates in them more compassion for the differences of others.

16. One important example of this is Nicholas Grier's book, *Care for the Mental and Spiritual Health of Black Men: Hope to Keep Going*, Religion and Race (Lanham, MD: Lexington Books, 2019).

17. Sheryl A. Kujawa-Holbrook, *A House of Prayer for All Peoples: Congregations Building Multiracial Community* (Bethesda, MD: Alban Institute, 2002).

Accepting the "and" empowers multiracial people to feel a greater sense of confidence as they live to overcome fixed boundaries that have been imposed upon them by hegemonic ideologies. Yet, if only multiracial people accept the "and," a new "either/or" is created. "Accepting the "and" is an expansive way of living that must creatively touch, include, and incorporate the entire world. This is not an easy process, for it requires courageous humility, forgiveness, and mercy. When it comes to racialized experiences in the United States, "accepting the 'and'" cannot be for individual gain but must establish new bonds of solidarity with others who experience racism and social oppression, beginning with Black and Indigenous peoples, and including other communities of color. Multiracial Cosmotheandrism is the spiritual work that multiracial people uniquely reveal in the domain of the "metapolitical"[18] as we "listen to all non-dominant cultures, inviting them to manifest themselves through their own natures and subjective identities to allow for a new kind of human being that has overcome haughtiness, fear, and ignorance."[19] Consequently, Multiracial Cosmotheandrism insists that knowledge about one another and our experiences is heart to heart—contextual, situational, and intimately spiritual—rather than done from a distance. In the spiritual life, opening oneself to the perspectives and experiences of others is crucial for spiritual maturity. This is what all great social movements have taught us. We need one another, and our freedom is bound up together; hence it can only be known when the Whole is included. We must accept the "and."

18. Raimon Panikkar, "Raimon Panikkar: The Foundations of Democracy and the Discovery of the Metapolitical," *Interculture* no. 136 (April 1999): 30.

19. Salvador Harguindey, "The Spirit of Politics," Integral World blog, https://www.integralworld.net.

Make Way for Mysticism

Mystical experience is not something reserved for the "chosen," "lucky," or those who have ridden themselves of all imperfections. It is something that does not come as a result of effort or willpower. It is a gift that mysteriously deepens through our participatory consent. Yet, what do we consent to if our spiritual awakening is not the result of our actions or based on merit? Our consent is a simple yes. A yes that is detached from outcomes and gives up attempts to manipulate or control life. We can discover our life only when we are ready to accept it in all of its beauty and pain. To experience that which ultimately fulfills and liberates us, we must acknowledge that this does not happen on our own terms. For this reason, Multiracial Cosmotheandrism asks that we *make way for mysticism* by slowly and gently beginning to allow the ego within us to die. While we cannot make this happen, we can consent to it happening mysteriously within us, empowered by that which is beyond us.

When we are open to this, we can grow in learning how to stabilize ourselves in mystical awareness. Multiracial Cosmotheandrism bears witness to a capacity for communion that is deeper than anything that words can express and allows for bonds to be made even when experiences are not shared, fully understood rationally, or even "feel gotten" empathically. However, this connection demands vulnerability with one another. The vulnerability necessary for mystical experience is the reason why we must "make way" for it. In Multiracial Cosmotheandrism, relationships are fostered on the mystical premise that each experience is irreplaceable, unrepeatable, and invaluable to our collective shared Life. In the solitude where we experience our personhood as intimately related with all others, multiraciality finds harmony with all of Reality. From the paradox of harmony amid our infinite particularities, respect, confidentiality, and compassion arise. In Multiracial Cosmotheandrism, our first response to the suffering or joy in the world is not to fix it or change it, but to "make way" for it so that we can receive it within ourselves first. In receiving the world, we join in on the work of transformation through loving presence. Multiracial Cosmotheandrism suggests a response of reverence that is characterized by tenderness, freedom, and playfulness so that we can live more fully alive and conscious of the Mystery.

The interrelatedness of Multiracial Cosmotheandrism privileges an openness to the ways that Mystery is always creatively at work, challenging our biases and assumptions, inviting bonds to emerge through the grounds of humility. Multiracial Cosmotheandrism resists imposing a strict set of definitions on what community should look like and recognizes that we all have something to contribute to our collective flourishing. We are to "make way" for this encounter because no singular approach will do.

Remember Raimon Panikkar

Remembrance is an important aspect of the Christian tradition. Panikkar evokes the importance of spiritual remembrance as he writes that the Eucharist "produces and effectively realizes the resurrection of the flesh."[20] From a Panikkarian perspective, to spiritually remember is also to accept death and impermanence; and, through this acceptance, welcome Resurrection Life. No longer alive, Panikkar's own life was made complete through *leaving*, through participating in trinitarian perichoresis, through making way for the Spirit to come again. In Multiracial Cosmotheandrism, we remember Raimon Panikkar neither to

20. Raimon Panikkar, *Christianity, Part One: The Christian Tradition*, ed. Milena Carrara Pavan (Maryknoll, NY: Orbis Books, 2015), 161.

immortalize him nor to encourage uncritical[21] imitation of him. Remembering Panikkar is to connect to his life as a transparent and unique *mediator* of Christ. Influenced by his own thought, we are not, then, looking to perpetuate the *bios* of his life but the *zoe* that passed through him, allowing for the divine that shone through him to ripple through us. When we remember him in this way, we receive new possibilities of creativity, healing, and beauty that otherwise would not have been if not for his life. Multiracial Cosmotheandrism calls for each person to participate in remembrance concretely by giving one's life away. It is a call to transcend the historical dimension and allow the All to flow, not holding onto anything, trusting in Reality itself for its continuation. While there is a real temptation to cling to Life in its many forms, remembering Panikkar must also allow him to go, so Life through the invisible Spirit can reappear again anew. In Multiracial Cosmotheandrism, Panikkar is remembered as a mixed-race person who bears witness to a Life that transcends race and racism while yet embracing the particularities of social identities and contingencies with a humble awareness of human experience. Panikkar becomes one who extends an invitation to realize the presence of the vast water at the depth dimension of Life, receiving yet transcending the sole drop.

Imagining an Incarnation of Multiracial Cosmotheandrism

Embracing the flow of *incarnatio continua*, I invite you to imagine a community that can embody Multiracial Cosmo-

21. Panikkar once quoted and revised the words of Antonio Machado, writing, "Pilgrim there is no path, you yourself are making it by walking! Take heed lest obedience and discipline go blind." See *A Dwelling Place for Wisdom* (Louisville, KY: Westminster-John Knox Press, 1993), 155.

theandrism. Imagine with me a group of diverse people who are radically honest with themselves and with one another. It is a group that embraces plurality and ends that are not neatly tied but still loose. Trust and compassion thrive at the core of this group. Imagine the joys and challenges of learning to accept the rich diversity of their lived experiences, including their joys and challenges. In sharing, they begin to recognize that they are each a microcosm of the whole, worthy of respect and care. This group does not romanticize the pains and horrors of existence, instead nourishing themselves and one another through a return to spiritual practices that tend to interiority.

Each of the members is committed to individual and collective spiritual practices that are both private and public and that cultivate nonjudgmental attentiveness and curiosity. Through rhythms of practice separately and together, they increase their capacities to be open to new forms of knowing and relating to one another. As they welcome each newness into themselves and the group, creativity is birthed in unforeseen ways that can mirror the unending, living flow of Life itself. A spirit of play and openness emanates from their being. While they remain radically aware of the systems in the world that produce harm and violence, they engage in the world's healing by being firmly committed to living alternatively in nonviolence together, in communion with one another and the cosmos at large.

They celebrate and remember the wisdom of the elements of materiality—fire, water, earth, and air—while paying attention to the small and still voice of the divine that could be found welling up in the mundane moments of their shared lives. This group honors limitations, apologizes and makes reparations when necessary. They learn to slowly embrace their humanity as a gift to enjoy in each day and mundane act, offering themselves and one another tenderness, gentleness, and mercy. The group prioritizes hospitality and welcomes guests with honor. They strive to de-center their assumptions, knowing that, in receptivity, transformation flows. They proclaim a reality of peace and liberation, not by waiting for it in another life but by becoming the living embodiments of those truths in their relationships together.

The community I describe could be waved off as wishful thinking, but imagining this group is a crucial move to imagine the new worlds of being through Multiracial Cosmotheandrism. New worlds become possible, and actualized, by practicing imaginative attention together. While so much of media, popular culture, and inherited ancestral patterns are trapped by monolithic and monocultural norms, Multiracial Cosmotheandrism invites a greater fullness of being to emerge through interdependent and diverse communion. Multiracial Cosmotheandrism bears possibilities of transformation at the personal level but also carries the potential for communal, organizational, and social-institutional change.

Further Implications

Practical Theology

Multiracial Cosmotheandrism encourages practical theology to pay attention to our world in important ways. This book has highlighted at least three significant areas that practical theologians must consider in our work moving forward. First, race, racism, and colonization in the lives of mixed-race people are critical influences on spiritual formation and spiritual care. Second, careful reflection on the role that digital technology can play in gathering, forming, and supporting others in their formation is vital in the twenty-first century. Third, I have shown how spiritual care is enhanced from shared contemplative practice, and practical theology is equipped to continue to attend to and promote this kind of relational care if it is willing to do so.

The first consideration assumes that race, racism, and racial oppression continue to hinder and harm the flourishing of all people who are living in lands that have been colonized. While one's racialized experiences are contingent based on a few contextual factors, the fact remains that race continues to be an essential component of consideration when addressing spirituality and spiritual practices that respond to colonization; even more so for mixed-race people who are largely invisible to racial justice efforts. While the temptation may be for race (along with other categories) to be treated as a static social identifier, this book advocates that race has many layers of complexity within it that involve power dynamics, other social identities, and a level of agency. Similarly, to how queer and trans studies have invited gender and sexuality to be complicated,[22] multiraciality invites us to treat race similarly. Therefore, if we are to better dismantle structures of oppression at large, we must continue to resist monolithic definitions of race and particularly center those who have experienced multiple minority racial status (especially those who have no background of being white) so that we may have a fuller picture of how race operationalizes.[23]

Additionally, because spirituality attempts to be holistically inclusive of life, it is vital that racial dynamics be interrogated regularly and consistently in spiritual programs. Based on the results of this study, it is essential that practical theology further explore how employing critical mixed-race studies in spiritual formation

22. Kylan Mattias de Vries and Carey Jean Sojka, "Transitioning Gender, Transitioning Race: Transgender People and Multiracial Positionality," *International Journal of Transgender Health*, November 8, 2020, 1–11.

23. David L. Brunsma, Daniel Delgado, and Kerry Ann Rockquemore, "Liminality in the Multiracial Experience: Towards a Concept of Identity Matrix," *Identities* 20, no. 5 (August 19, 2013): 481–502.

programs can help participants heal in more holistic ways and, alternatively, how such an integration of interdisciplinary critical studies can help others imagine new ways of relating to one another. Doing spiritual work in ways that are conscious of societal oppression better ensures that historically dominant ways of being are not unconsciously re-enacted. There have been too many cases where people leave the "real world" to meditate and never question how they might be complicit with racial injustice. In my program, I used the wisdom of critical mixed-race studies as the starting point for the invitation to practice contemplation. What if more spiritual programming started with a more nuanced understanding of race—along with how race is connected to other experiences of oppression—as the first step taken toward a life committed to anti-oppression in all forms?

The second consideration for practical theology moving forward is the roles that digital and electronic technologies play in individual and community formation. When privileging a Cosmotheandric understanding of creative freedom, can digital community be a viable way to convene those who are marginalized in the world to offer support and spiritual renewal? If so, what are the best practices to this end? Jaume Agustí Cullell influences my own thought in this area:

> The awareness of the creative freedom of all reality should be the context where science and technology develop their proper creative freedom. They should help implant and enlarge, and not impede or supplant, the other forms of creative freedom, of both people and the things themselves.[24]

24. Jaume Agustí Cullell, "From Scientific Experiment to Whole Experience through Freedom," in Kala Acharya et al., eds., *Fullness of Life* (Mumbai: Somaiya Publications, 2008), 288.

The qualitative research that I performed would have been nearly impossible to complete if I had not had the ability to perform it virtually. The population with whom I was working was geographically dispersed, did not have the financial means to gather in one place, and they were the only mixed-race people in their immediate geographical contexts. Through digital technologies, I was able to organize the group, share in spiritual practices together, and create robust dialogue about their life experiences. Further, completing the program virtually also meant that people had an opportunity to stay consistent with their own natural and organic settings rather than being extracted out of it, where dynamics would necessarily change. How can practical theology use technology in ways that promote natural rhythms of rest and relationality and foster an increased sensitivity to creative freedom in their home settings? After evaluating the program, it was clear that there needs to be more attention given to the unique role that technology plays in our formation as well as the best ways it can be used to cultivate spiritual awareness, to build trust, intimacy, and connection. As digital technologies become more prevalent, practical theology can benefit from a Cosmotheandric approach.

Third, a critical finding of this study is that spiritual care can be deepened through what I call contemplative community practice. While others have attested to how contemplative practice complements the work of spiritual care in one-on-one settings, and even the need for replenishing the soul of the care-provider, this program showed how a community practicing contemplation together[25] can build a powerful container of support that

25. My work especially focused on how community care can address issues of race and racism and how a collectivist approach to spiritual formation can better support multiracial populations with their ongoing experiences of systemic oppression.

extends way beyond the role of a single care-provider. Further consideration could be given to ask what best practices are for a facilitator who is relying on contemplative approaches to interact and provide care for those who are presently being socially oppressed. Because spiritual care has long been centered on ways of healing, more investigation around contemplative community-care practices would be of great benefit.

Finally, this study suggests that these considerations are all intertwined. The insights that Multiracial Cosmotheandrism offers emerge from the ways that MCAM and its participants engaged race as a dynamic and complex factor, digital pedagogies in spiritual formation, and contemplative shared practices within community together. Attending to these factors and how they influence each other could strengthen approaches to care for minoritized communities and populations for the long haul.

Critical Mixed-Race Studies

This book also has implications and offers questions for the growth of CMRS, a field committed to complexifying analyses of race so that more expansive and holistic efforts for racial justice can be enacted. The first implications are the profound ways that practical theology and spirituality can provide resources for racial justice beyond mere rational or intellectual analysis. The second implication is the importance of centering the joys and wisdoms of mixed-race people.

One of the major insights from a practical theology of multiraciality is that the transformation of racism cannot come from logic or reason alone. Multiracial Cosmotheandrism is a way of being in the world that prioritizes the qualitative energy of relational presence even as it does communicate information about the world. Multiracial Cosmotheandrism relies on spiritual characteristics such as compassion, humility, and interconnectedness at the center of racial healing. When considering CMRS from a practical theological lens, one is asked to view oppression in ways that include but also move beyond a theoretical and rational lens and center the lived experiences and stories that come from resilience, creativity, and beauty. With the characteristic both/and posture of CMRS, people who are theologically committed to anti-racism recognize challenge alongside beauty, acquiring newfound strength to continue in the long work of racial justice. Taking a practical theological and, more specifically, contemplative approach to CMRS more thoroughly identifies the various ways in which racism insidiously operates and creates a more profound container where experiences of all kinds are welcomed and invited.

Multiracial Cosmotheandrism can open CMRS to embrace spirituality and spiritual diversity in its analyses. What are other spiritualities that can guide further studies in CMRS in the spirit of inclusion? What other resources can come from practical theology or spirituality so that the actions that CMRS intends to galvanize can be strengthened, resourced, and sustained? Multiracial Cosmotheandrism challenges CMRS to further integrate practical theological approaches to multiraciality in its broad coalition of study.

The second implication enhances a characteristic commitment of CMRS. Multiracial Cosmotheandrism echoes and advances the commitment to anti-oppressive ways of living and being in the world by telling more stories of how mixed-race people are flourishing in spite of racism and monoracism. While CMRS is deftly able to name, identify, and expose racism and monoracial bias, spiritual care in the pattern of Multiracial Cosmotheandrism centers multiracial well-being and can be a resource that raises up the lived experiences of others who are finding wholeness in the midst of a racialized world. While one cannot remain naïve and only focus on the positive side, attending to joy is a habit of resistance that builds resilience. Neither idealistic nor nihilistic, CMRS could benefit from the findings and intuitions of spiritual care that are committed to identifying the joy and beauty of life amid its frailties. Embracing life's joys can, in turn, revitalize and restore people, empowering them to take necessary actions to help alleviate the suffering caused by racism.

Panikkar Studies

The most important contribution that this book makes is its support for living in spiritual freedom. The heart of Panikkarian studies is the admission that "freedom is the fruit of the experience of the free gift of Life."[26] Panikkar's life ought to be understood as an invitation to each of us to live more *authentically* and *spiritually liberated,* aligned with the *ontonomic* structure of Reality. "True freedom is not a predetermined path" but is found where fear is overcome and the temptation to "imitate any model" is resisted. Freedom is "something brand new; it is my inspiration, my creation, something that comes from within and which I myself do not know how to live out," Panikkar said.[27]

This book reflects a pilgrimage that I took with others toward this freedom and contributes uniquely to the *incarnatio continua* in ways that, like Panikkar's own life, will not be fully contained in its words. The findings I have shared are not "perfect" and could not have been pre-planned but were forged through a process of contemplation. I hope that this book paves the way for other Panikkar scholars to join in this symphony for free-

26. Raimon Panikkar, *The Water of the Drop: Fragments from Panikkar's Diaries*, ed. Milena Carrara Pavan (Delhi: Indian Society for Promoting Christian Knowledge, 2018), 79.

27. Panikkar, *A Dwelling Place for Wisdom*, 100.

dom with their own melodic contribution. With Scott Eastham, I believe that studies of Panikkar, his life and work, need to be "maverick" inquiries that cultivate "creativity, spontaneity, and improvisation, letting the labels fall where they may" as we explore the uncharted waters that flow in the depths of Being.[28] Particularly for others in North America who have been marginalized and oppressed by colonization and racism, engaging Panikkar's life, philosophy, and mysticism can encourage a return to contemplation as a primary theological method that strengthens our capacities to engage the world in transformative ways.

In North America, the spaces where multiracial people can meaningfully engage their spiritualities for healing and well-being are sparse. The impact of a Panikkarian intercultural and mystical approach to multiraciality cannot be understated. As multiple catastrophes continue to unfold in our world, the call to heal and re-create the world is needed now more than ever. Our present conditions demand that we find important guidance within our traditions and that we strike out on completely unpredictable and new paths forward. Panikkar scholars, critical mixed-race scholars, spiritual practitioners, and multiracial people must abide in the cosmic confidence to which Panikkar bore witness; a confidence that "cannot be put into words. Nor does it need to be. It needs to be lived."[29] With immense gratitude, let us live more alive and more aware of the Mystery that permeates multiraciality through and through. With immense compassion, let us experience a renewed hope. With immense inspiration, let us transform the violence of this world through wisdom and love. May it be so.

28. Eastham, *Dreaming a New Earth*, 37.

29. G. Hall, "Cosmic Confidence and Global Peace," in *Raimon Panikkar: His Legacy and Vision*, ed. K. Acharya and M. C. Pavan (Mumbai: Somaiya Publications, 2008).

Appendix A

The Qualitative Research Design

MCAM lasted a total of four weeks and involved the following aspects of formation: a weekly live, online video session featuring both teaching and discussion, guided meditations, and written personal and group reflections.[1] In gathering the data, I utilized a mix of pastoral ethnographic,[2] participatory action, and orientational inquiry qualitative methods.[3] All of these were informed by decolonial[4] methodological commitments as I, being mixed-race myself, sought to join multiracial participants in their material and psychological struggle for liberation from the deadly effects of racial oppression and colonization.

1. For a more thorough understanding of my approach to facilitating group formation around spirituality and spiritual care, please see the article I wrote entitled "Decolonizing Pastoral Care in the Classroom: An Invitation to a Pedagogy of Spirit Experience," *Teaching Theology & Religion* 24, no. 2 (June 2021): 107–16.

2. Michael Quinn Patton, *Qualitative Research & Evaluation Methods: Integrating Theory and Practice*, 4th ed. (Thousand Oaks, CA: Sage Publications, 2015).

3. Mary Moschella, "Practice Matters: New Directions in Ethnography and Qualitative Research," in *Pastoral Theology and Care: Critical Trajectories in Theory and Practice,* ed. Jack Ramsay (Hoboken, NJ: John Wiley & Sons, 2018), 8–10.

4. Linda Tuhiwai Smith, *Decolonizing Methodologies: Research and Indigenous Peoples*, 2nd ed. (London: Zed Books, 2012).

Finding Participants

I invited only those who identify as multiracial (as defined in the earlier chapters of the book) to be part of the program. Participant recruitment was done via personal relationships as well as personal recommendations from university colleagues. The participants' involvement was voluntary, and, as an incentive, they were offered a $25 gift card to be received at the end of the study. Participants were required to have access to a working computer and stable internet connection, to be at least eighteen years of age, and to self-identify as multiracial. There were seven participants in all, and they were primarily nonwhite mixed with white (five participants). Two of the participants, however, were like me, of double-minority racial status.[5] While much of my research and preparation was formulated with double minorities in mind, the material we covered was generally applicable. More attention to the fluidity of whiteness could have been advantageous. When transcribing the data, I changed their names for purposes of confidentiality but included their academic year, age, and racial identity. The table in Appendix B shows a bit of the diversity represented in the program.

Recognizing Limits

While the program was open to those from any geographic location within the United States, all participants lived in Southern California. Each of the participants was also predisposed and pre-inclined to a space that centered spirituality, race, and social justice, with a clear self-identified interest in exploring their own lived mixed-race experiences in light of these factors. Therefore,

5. The complete demographic information on the group can be found in Appendix B.

the findings and conclusions of this study should be viewed as tentative and questioning as they emerge from people who are already interested in the intersections of race, social justice, and spirituality.

It is also important to note that each of these participants had never previously discussed race in their family upbringings. For the participants in this study, it was their first deep dive into talking about race, racism, and multi/racial experience(s). As I thought more about this, I wondered what it might have looked like to adapt the program content based on the pre-interviews, offering more foundational teachings on race and racism as well as mysticism and spirituality for them to review before we began. Additionally, although the data is drawn from people representative across economic, age, and racial/ethnic diversity, all participants were current students at predominantly white and Christian universities.

My analysis was done from an emic perspective, as I identify as a multiracial person and contemplative practitioner myself, and I acknowledge the ways in which my personal social location is implicated in the evaluative process. To further clarify my own social location, I identify as a heterosexual, cisgender, Christian, middle-class male, and a Hakka Malaysian Chinese Mexican American multiracial person of color with varying axes of privilege and oppression. I disclose these various social identifiers in my firm commitment to the practical theological framework of advocacy, which aims to give preferential voice to the experiences of multiracial people themselves, not just my own thoughts about it, and tying all insights back to their lived experiences.[6]

6. John W. Creswell, *30 Essential Skills for the Qualitative Researcher* (Thousand Oaks, CA: Sage Publications, 2016).

Analyzing the Data

To begin analysis, I collected qualitative data from the program in the following ways: semi-structured pre- and post-program interviews that lasted forty-five minutes each, participants' written reflections, participatory observation notes, and analytic journal notes.[7] All names were changed and not spoken during the recording. Interviews took place both before and after the program and were approximately 45 minutes in length. The participants signed an Informed Consent Form prior to their involvement with the study and were given permission to share any questions or concerns about the process. With the participants, I emphasized that there was no expectation that their experiences should fit into any prescribed boxes and asked them to challenge anything that was presented in the plenary sessions, videos, or spiritual practices. All participants elected to participate freely and were never expected to complete all elements of the program. In my commitment to consent and freedom, participants were also aware they could withdraw at any time, for any reason, without penalty or repercussion.

As I reviewed in the book, a practical theological, spiritual, and qualitative method was adopted in the design and analysis of this project that privileged a phenomenological approach. My goal in this approach was to focus on supporting participants' lived experience, in this case their racialized experiences, and to first report back the essence of what they shared before doing any other evaluation.[8] This gave me the best chance to hear the participants on their own terms and to offer multiple pathways for multiracial persons that might promote healing in their lives in ways that feel right to them. A phenomenological approach also

7. A set of the interview questions I used can be found in Appendix B.
8. Creswell, *30 Essential Skills.*

emphasizes the uniqueness of each participant to better understand two things: (1) the intersectional and personal workings of each participant, and (2) how MCAM supports them in engaging issues of race at personal, interpersonal, and systemic levels. I had four guiding questions that animated how I related to the data:

1. Does MCAM contribute to increased awareness of one's own lived experiences?
2. Does MCAM contribute to increased awareness of interconnectedness to diverse others?
3. Does MCAM contribute to increased awareness of systemic racism and racialization?
4. Does MCAM offer tools and resources that promote healing and intercultural reconciliation?

To organize the data around these questions, I elected two primary coding methods known as *a priori* and *in vivo*.[9] *A priori* codes were created initially to sort data with pre-determined themes that come from critical mixed-race studies and practical theology. In this study, there were twelve *a priori* codes that related to the four questions that I initially took into the analysis. *In vivo* coding is done to keep participants' actual words at the center of the analysis process.[10] I found that *a priori* codes were helpful to assess the effectiveness of MCAM, and *in vivo* coding was key to highlighting aspects of the participants' experience that presented both challenges to the program as well as previously unrecognized affirmations.

9. A set of the codes that I used to analyze the data can be found in Appendix D.

10. Creswell, *30 Essential Skills*.

Appendix B. Demographic Information of Participants						
Name	*Age*	*Gender*	*Religious affiliation, if any*	*Ethnicity*	*Racial self-identification*	*Sexual Orientation*
Faye	24	Female	Christian	Chinese and Mexican	Asian and Hispanic	Heterosexual
Ellie	22	Female	Catholic	White	Hispanic and White	Heterosexual
Molly	20	Female	Christian	White and Filipina	White and Filipina	Heterosexual
Brooklyn	20	Female	Pentecostal	Caucasian and Caribbean	Biracial	Heterosexual
Blaire	22	Female	Non-religious	Hispanic and Latina	Biracial	Heterosexual
Will	19	Male	Christian	Black and White	Mixed	Heterosexual
Sean	24	Male	Christian and Hindu	Puerto Rican and East Indian	Hispanic	Heterosexual

Appendix C

Interview Questions

Semi-Structured Interview Questions: **How do you relate to race personally and socially?**

- Topic: Relating to Race
  - How would you define and describe "race"?
  - How was "race" discussed in your upbringing? Family? Community?
  - How does "race" affect society at large?
    - • How does race affect your personal life?
  - I am curious how you would describe your own racial identity?
  - What does being ______ or "multiracial" or "mixed" mean to you?
    - • When did you first realize you were "mixed"?
  - Does race affect other aspects of your social identity?
    - • Gender, socio-economic status, ability, spirituality, citizenship
  - What approaches do you take when race comes up in various social settings?
    - • Friends and family, school, work, online, spiritual community?
  - Any needs, wants, or desires to better relate to race personally?

- Topic: Spirituality
  - What does spirituality mean to you?
  - What is one example of a significant spiritual experience in your life?
    - Why do you see this experience as spiritual?
  - How does your spirituality inform the way you engage race in the United States?
    - Are there any particular actions your spirituality has led you to take?

Post-Interview: **How has MCAM impacted how you relate to race personally and socially?**

- Topic: Race
  - How do you understand "race" today?
  - How does "race" affect life in the United States?
    - How do you see your past upbringing and the ways race impacted it?
    - How does race affect your experience in US society today?
  - What does being multiracial or "mixed" mean to you?
  - How do you understand race to impact other aspects of your social identity?
    - Gender, socio-economic status, ability, spirituality, citizenship
  - Are there any perceived personal needs that would enable you to relate to race in a more life-giving way?

- Topic: Spirituality
  - How would you define spirituality?
  - What is a recent spiritual experience you have had?
    - Why would you define it as spiritual?

- How does your spirituality inform your understanding of the category of race?
- What approach do you anticipate taking when race comes up in the future?
    - Around friends and family, school, work, online, spiritual community
- What questions did you leave our experience with?
    - Any closing comments, suggestions, or affirmations on the process?

Appendix D

Coding Scheme

A priori codes

1. Psychological and emotional self-awareness
2. Body awareness
3. Human as community
4. Transcendent connectedness
5. Internalization of racial oppression
6. Racism is fluid and contextual
7. Intersectionality
8. Racialization is ordinary to US society and life
9. Self-identified needs
10. Self-empowered creative action
11. Culturally integrative (social location and biases)
12. Holistic/multidimensional care

In vivo codes

13. Race avoidance
14. Perceived dangers of "race"
15. "What are you?"
16. Open spiritualities

Bibliography

Althaus-Reid, Marcella. *The Queer God*. New York: Routledge, 2003.

Amaladass, Anand. "Panikkar's Quest for an Alternative Way of Thinking and Acting." In *Raimon Panikkar: Intercultural and Interreligious Dialogue*. Edited by Joan Vergés Gifra, 49–69. Noms de La Filosofia Catalana 12. Girona: Documenta Universitaria, 2017.

Anzaldúa, Gloria. *Borderlands: The New Mestiza = La Frontera*. 1st ed. San Francisco: Spinsters/Aunt Lute, 1987.

Austen, Ian. "Unmarked Graves at Residential Schools in Canada: What to Know—The New York Times." https://www.nytimes.com/2021/06/07/world/canada/mass-graves-residential-schools.html.

Baeumer, Bettina. Introduction to *Raimundo Panikkar: A Pilgrim across Worlds*. Edited by Kapila Vatsyayan and Côme Carpentier de Gourdon, 11–15. New Delhi: Niyogi Books, 2016.

Barnes, Michael, SJ. "Neither Myself nor Another—the Interreligious Belonging of Raimon Panikkar." In *Hindu-Christian Dual Belonging*. Edited by Daniel Soars and Nadya Pohran, 33–50. 1st ed. London: Routledge, 2022. https://doi.org/10.4324/9781003142591–3.

Barnett, Brooke, and Peter Felten, eds. *Intersectionality in Action: A Guide for Faculty and Campus Leaders for Creating Inclusive Classrooms and Institutions*. 1st ed. Sterling, VA: Stylus Publishing, 2016.

Bell, Derrick A. *Faces at the Bottom of the Well: The Permanence of Racism*. New York: Basic Books, 1992.

Berger, Michele Tracy, and Kathleen Guidroz, eds. *The Intersectional Approach: Transforming the Academy through Race, Class, and Gender.* Chapel Hill: University of North Carolina Press, 2009.

Bourgeault, Cynthia. "Christophany by Raimon Panikkar," 2012, 6.

Browning, Don S. *A Fundamental Practical Theology: Descriptive and Strategic Proposals.* Minneapolis: Fortress Press, 1991.

Brunsma, David L., Daniel Delgado, and Kerry Ann Rockquemore. "Liminality in the Multiracial Experience: Towards a Concept of Identity Matrix." *Identities* 20, no. 5 (August 19, 2013): 481–502. https://doi.org/10.1080/1070289X.2013.827576.

Burghardt, Walter J. "Contemplation: A Long Loving Look at the Real." *Church,* no. 5 (Winter 1989): 10.

Butler, Judith. *Gender Trouble: Feminism and the Subversion of Identity.* Routledge Classics. New York: Routledge, 2006.

Cahalan, Kathleen A., and Gordon S. Mikoski, eds. *Opening the Field of Practical Theology: An Introduction.* Lanham, MD: Rowman & Littlefield, 2014.

Cameron, Helen, ed. *Talking about God in Practice: Theological Action Research and Practical Theology.* London: SCM Press, 2010.

Carter, J. Kameron. *Race: A Theological Account.* Oxford: Oxford University Press, 2008.

Coates, Ta-Nehisi. *Between the World and Me.* New York: Random House, 2015.

Conde-Frazier, Elizabeth, S. Steve Kang, and Gary A. Parrett. *A Many Colored Kingdom: Multicultural Dynamics for Spiritual Formation.* Grand Rapids, MI: Baker Academic, 2004.

Cornille, Catherine. "Religious Hybridity and Christian Identity: Promise and Problem." *Currents in Theology and Mission* 48, no. 1 (2021). http://www.currentsjournal.org.

Cousins, Ewert. "Uniting Human, Cosmic and Divine." *America,* January 1, 2007. https://www.americamagazine.org/issue/598/bookings/uniting-human-cosmic-and-divine.

Coward, Harold G. "Panikkar's Approach to Interreligious Dialogue." *CrossCurrents* 29, no. 2 (1979): 183–92.

Crenshaw, Kimberlé. "Demarginalizing the Intersection of Race & Sex: A Black Feminist Critique of Antidiscrimination Doctrine, Feminist Theory, and Antiracist Politics [1989]." In *Feminist Legal Theory*. Edited by Katharine T. Bartlett and Rosanne Kennedy, 57–80. 1st ed. London: Routledge, 1991. https://doi.org/10.4324/9780429500480-5.

Crenshaw, Kimberlé, ed. *Critical Race Theory: The Key Writings That Formed the Movement*. New York: New Press, 1995.

Creswell, John W. *30 Essential Skills for the Qualitative Researcher*. Thousand Oaks, CA: Sage Publications, 2016.

———. *Research Design: Qualitative, Quantitative, and Mixed Methods Approaches*. 3rd ed. Thousand Oaks, CA: Sage Publications, 2009.

Cullel, Jaume Agustí. "From Scientific Experiment to Whole Experience through Freedom." In *Fullness of Life*. Edited by Kala Acharya, Milena Carrara Pavan, and William Parker, 285–308. Mumbai: Somaiya Publications, 2008.

Curington, Celeste Vaughan. "Rethinking Multiracial Formation in the United States: Toward an Intersectional Approach." *Sociology of Race and Ethnicity* 2, no. 1 (January 2016): 27–41. https://doi.org/10.1177/2332649215591864.

DaCosta, Kimberly A. "Multiracial Categorization, Identity, and Policy in (Mixed) Racial Formations." *Annual Review of Sociology* 46, no. 1 (July 30, 2020): 335–53. https://doi.org/10.1146/annurev-soc-121919–054649.

Dallmayr, Fred R. "Sacred Secularity and Prophetism: A Tension in Panikkar's Work?" In *Raimon Panikkar: A Companion to His Life and Thought*. Edited by Peter Phan and Young-chan Ro, 235–41. Cambridge, UK: James Clarke, 2020.

———. *Spiritual Guides: Pathfinders in the Desert*. Notre Dame, IN: University of Notre Dame Press, 2017.

Daniel, G. Reginald. Foreword to *Multiracial Experiences in Higher Education: Contesting Knowledge, Honoring Voice, and Innovating Practice*. Sterling, VA: Stylus Publishing, 2021.

Daniel, G. Reginald, Laura Kina, Wei Ming Dariotis, and Camilla Fojas. "Emerging Paradigms in Critical Mixed Race Studies," *Journal of Critical Mixed Race Studies* 1, no. 1 (2014): 61. https://doi.org/10.5070/C811013868.

Davenport, Lauren D. *Politics beyond Black and White.* Cambridge: Cambridge University Press, 2018. http://public.eblib.com/choice/publicfullrecord.aspx?p=5330489.

De La Torre, Miguel A., ed. *Faith and Reckoning after Trump.* Maryknoll, NY: Orbis Books, 2021.

Delgado, Richard, and Jean Stefancic. *The Derrick Bell Reader.* Critical America. New York: New York University Press, 2005.

Eastham, Scott. "After Panikkar." In *Dreaming a New Earth: Raimon Panikkar and Indigenous Spiritualities.* Edited by Gerard Hall and Joan Hendriks, 24–40. Preston, Victoria (Australia): Mosaic Press, 2013.

Ferrer, Jorge N., and Jacob H. Sherman, eds. *The Participatory Turn: Spirituality, Mysticism, Religious Studies.* Albany: State University of New York Press, 2008.

Finley, James. "Transforming Trauma Recordings." *James Finley* (blog). https://jamesfinley.org/ish.

Foor, Daniel. *Ancestral Medicine: Rituals for Personal and Family Healing.* Rochester, VT: Bear & Company, 2017.

Foster-Frau, Sylvia, Ted Mellnik, and Adrian Blanco. "Mixed-Race Americans Are Fastest-Growing Racial Group, Census Shows." *Washington Post,* October 8, 2021. https://www.washingtonpost.com/nation/2021/10/08/mixed-race-americans-increase-census/.

Frohlich, Mary. "Spirit, Spirituality, and Contemplative Method." *Spiritus: A Journal of Christian Spirituality* 20, no. 1 (2020): 31–44. https://doi.org/10.1353/scs.2020.0019.

Fundació Vivarium Raimon Panikkar. "Raimon Panikkar Official Site." https://www.raimon-panikkar.org/english/home.html.

Gaskins, Pearl Fuyo. *What Are You? Voices of Mixed-Race Young People.* New York: Henry Holt, 1999.

Gibbs, Philip. "Indigenous Spirituality: Expanding the View." In *Dreaming a New Earth: Raimon Panikkar and Indigenous*

Spiritualities. Edited by Gerard Hall and Joan Hendriks, 54–66. Preston, Victoria (Australia): Mosaic Press, 2013.

Giri, Ananta Kumar, ed. *Roots, Routes and a New Awakening: Beyond One and Many and Alternative Planetary Futures*. Singapore: Palgrave Macmillan, 2021.

Gispert-Sauch, George. "Raimon Panikkar: Prophet of Samanvaya." In *Raimundo Panikkar: A Pilgrim across Worlds*. Edited by Kapila Vatsyayan and Côme Carpentier de Gourdon, 127–34. New Delhi: Niyogi Books, 2016.

Graham, Elaine. "Is Practical Theology a Form of 'Action Research'?" *International Journal of Practical Theology* 17, no. 1 (January 2013). https://doi.org/10.1515/ijpt-2013–0010.

Grier, Nicholas. *Care for the Mental and Spiritual Health of Black Men: Hope to Keep Going*. Religion and Race. Lanham, MD: Lexington Books, 2019.

Hall, Gerard. "Cosmic Confidence and Global Peace." In *Fullness of Life*. Edited by Kala Acharya, Milena Carrara Pavan, and William Parker, 307–29. Mumbai: Somaiya Publications, 2008.

———. "Raimon Panikkar: The Human Person" (2018), 39. https://gerardhallsm.files.wordpress.com/2018/08/panikkar_the-human-person.pdf.

Hall, Gerard, and Joan Hendriks. *Dreaming a New Earth: Raimon Panikkar and Indigenous Spiritualities*. Preston, Victoria (Australia): Mosaic Press, 2013.

Harguindey, Salvador. "The Spirit of Politics." https://www.integralworld.net/es/salvador3.html.

Harris, Jessica C. "Multiracial College Students' Experiences with Multiracial Microaggressions." *Race Ethnicity and Education* 20, no. 4 (July 4, 2017): 429–45. https://doi.org/10.1080/13613324.2016.1248836.

———. "Toward a Critical Multiracial Theory in Education." *International Journal of Qualitative Studies in Education* 29, no. 6 (July 2, 2016): 795–813. https://doi.org/10.1080/09518398.2016.1162870.

Harris, Jessica C., Allison BrckaLorenz, and Thomas F. Nelson

Laird. "Engaging in the Margins: Exploring Differences in Biracial Students' Engagement by Racial Heritage." *Journal of Student Affairs Research and Practice* 55, no. 2 (April 3, 2018): 137–54. https://doi.org/10.1080/19496591.2018.1406364.

Harris, Jessica C., and Z. Nicolazzo. "Navigating the Academic Borderlands as Multiracial and Trans* Faculty Members." *Critical Studies in Education* 61, no. 2 (March 14, 2020): 229–44. https://doi.org/10.1080/17508487.2017.1356340.

Hill Collins, Patricia, and Sirma Bilge. *Intersectionality.* Key Concepts Series. Malden, MA: Polity Press, 2016.

Holmes, Barbara. *Crisis Contemplation: Healing the Wounded Village.* Albuquerque, NM: Center of Action and Contemplation, 2021.

Holmes, Barbara, and Donny Bryant. "The Cosmic We with Barbara Holmes and Donny Bryant on Apple Podcasts." https://podcasts.apple.com/us/podcast/the-cosmic-we-with-barbara-holmes-and-donny-bryant/id1579447917.

hooks, bell. *Feminist Theory: From Margin to Center.* 3rd ed. London: Routledge, 1984. https://doi.org/10.4324/9781315 743172.

Hübl, Thomas. *Healing Collective Trauma: A Process for Integrating Our Intergenerational & Cultural Wounds.* Boulder, CO: Sounds True, 2020.

Ifekwunigwe, Jayne O., ed. *"Mixed Race" Studies: A Reader.* New York: Routledge, 2004.

Jennings, Willie James. *The Christian Imagination: Theology and the Origins of Race.* New Haven: Yale University Press, 2010.

Johnston-Guerrero, Marc P., and Kevin Nadal. "Multiracial Microaggressions: Exposing Monoracism in Everyday Life and Clinical Practice." In *Microaggressions and Marginality.* Edited by Derald Wing Sue. Hoboken, NJ: John Wiley, 2010. https://www.academia.edu/363221/Multiracial_Microaggressions_Exposing_Monoracism_in_Everyday_Life_and_Clinical_Practice.

Johnston-Guerrero, Marc P., Charmaine Wijeyesinghe, and G. Reginald Daniel, eds. *Multiracial Experiences in Higher*

Education: Contesting Knowledge, Honoring Voice, and Innovating Practice. 1st ed. Sterling, VA: Stylus Publishing, 2021.

Kim-Cragg, HyeRan. *Interdependence: A Postcolonial Feminist Practical Theology.* Eugene, OR: Pickwick Publications, 2018.

King-O'Riain, Rebecca C., Stephen Small, Minelle Mahtani, Miri Song, and Paul Spickard, eds. *Global Mixed Race.* New York: New York University Press, 2014. https://doi.org/10.18574/nyu/9780814770733.001.0001.

Kluckhohn, Clyde, and Henry Murray. *Personality in Nature, Society, and Culture.* New York: Alfred A. Knopf, 1953.

Kohli, Rita, and Daniel G. Solórzano. "Teachers, Please Learn Our Names! Racial Microaggressions and the K–12 Classroom." *Race Ethnicity and Education* 15, no. 4 (September 2012): 441–62. https://doi.org/10.1080/13613324.2012.674026.

Kujawa-Holbrook, Sheryl A. *A House of Prayer for All Peoples: Congregations Building Multiracial Community.* Lanham, MD: Rowman & Littlefield, 2003.

Kyle, Eric J. *Living Spiritual Praxis: Foundations for Spiritual Formation Program Development.* Eugene, OR: Pickwick Publications, 2013.

———. *Sacred Systems: Exploring Personal Transformation in the Western Christian Tradition.* Eugene, OR: Pickwick Publications, 2014.

Lartey, Emmanuel Yartekwei. *In Living Color: An Intercultural Approach to Pastoral Care and Counseling.* 2nd ed. New York: Jessica Kingsley Publishers, 2003.

Machado, Antonio. "Traveler, There Is No Path!" https://www.aspeninstitute.org/wp-content/uploads/2020/04/Machado_Traveler-There-Is-No-Path.pdf.

Magee, Rhonda V. *The Inner Work of Racial Justice: Healing Ourselves and Transforming Our Communities through Mindfulness.* New York: TarcherPerigee, 2019.

Manuel, Zenju Earthlyn. *The Way of Tenderness: Awakening through Race, Sexuality, and Gender.* Boston: Wisdom Publications, 2015.

McKibbin, Molly Littlewood. *Shades of Gray: Writing the New American Multiracialism*. Borderlands and Transcultural Studies. Lincoln: University of Nebraska Press, 2018.

Mehta, Nihun. "Compassion as a Basic Global Ethic | Service Space.Org," August 31, 2014. https://www.servicespace.org/blog/view.php?id=15497.

Merton, Thomas. "Thomas Merton's Letter to a Young Activist—Jim and Nancy Forest." https://jimandnancyforest.com/2014/10/mertons-letter-to-a-young-activist.

Mills, Charles W. *The Racial Contract*. Ithaca, NY: Cornell University Press, 2011.

Moschella, Mary C. "Practice Matters: New Directions in Ethnography and Qualitative Research." In *Pastoral Theology and Care: Critical Trajectories in Theory and Practice*. Edited by Nancy J. Ramsay, 8–10. Hoboken, NJ: John Wiley & Sons, 2018.

"Multiracial Americans: Counting America's Population | Pew Research Center." https://www.pewresearch.org/social-trends/2015/06/11/chapter-2–counting-multiracial-americans/.

Newman, Alyssa M. "Revisiting the Marginal Man: Bridging Immigration Scholarship and Mixed-Race Studies." *Sociology of Race and Ethnicity* 7, no. 1 (January 1, 2021): 26–40. https://doi.org/10.1177/2332649220933302.

Nojeim, Michael J. *Gandhi and King: The Power of Nonviolent Resistance*. Westport, CT: Praeger, 2004.

Olson, Kate. "Living the New Story." *Fetzer Institute*, 2012. https://fetzer.org.

Panikkar, Raimon. *The following list cites the titles in Panikkar's Opera Omnia. Full bibliographical information for the titles cited in this volume follow this listing.*

Opera Omnia. Edited by Milena Carrara Pavan. Maryknoll, NY: Orbis Books, 2018–2022

I. *Mysticism and Spirituality* (2 vols.)

Part 1: Mysticism, Fullness of Life

Part 2: Spirituality, the Way of Life

II. *Religion and Religions*

III. *Christianity* (2 vols.)
Part 1: The Christian Tradition (1961–1967)
Part 2: A Christophany
IV. *Hinduism* (2 vols.)
Part 1: The Vedic Experience: Mantramanjari
Part 2: The Dharma of India
V. *Buddhism*
VI. *Cultures and Religions in Dialogue* (2 vols.)
Part 1: Pluralism and Interculturality
Part 2: Intercultural and Interreligious Dialogue
VII. *Hinduism and Christianity*
VIII. *Trinitarian and Cosmotheandric Vision*
IX. *Mystery and Hermeneutics* (2 vols.)
Part 1: Myth, Symbol, and Ritual
Part 2: Faith, Hermeneutics, and Word
X. *Philosophy and Theology* (2 vols.)
Part 1: The Rhythm of Being
Part 2: Philosophical and Theological Thought
XI. *Sacred Secularity*
XII. *Space, Time, and Science*

———. *Christianity. Part Two: A Christophany.* Edited by Milena Carrara Pavan. Maryknoll, NY: Orbis Books, 2015.

———. *Christophany: The Fullness of Man.* Faith Meets Faith. Maryknoll, NY: Orbis Books, 2004.

———. *Cultural Disarmament: The Way to Peace.* Louisville, KY: Westminster-John Knox Press, 1995.

———. *Cultures and Religions in Dialogue. Part One: Pluralism and Interculturality.* Edited by Milena Carrara Pavan. Maryknoll, NY: Orbis Books, 2018.

———. *Cultures and Religions in Dialogue. Part Two: Intercultural and Interreligious Dialogue.* Edited by Milena Carrara Pavan. Maryknoll, NY: Orbis Books, 2018.

———. *A Dwelling Place for Wisdom.* 1st ed. Louisville, KY: Westminster/John Knox Press, 1993.

———. "Eruption of Truth: An Interview with Raimon Panikkar—Religion Online." https://www.religion-online.org/article/eruption-of-truth-an-interview-with-raimon-panikkar/.

———. "Human Dialogue and Religious Inter-Independence: Fire and Crystal." *Faith and Development*, January 2003.

———. *The Intrareligious Dialogue*. Rev. ed. New York: Paulist Press, 1999.

———. *Invisible Harmony: Essays on Contemplation and Responsibility*. Minneapolis: Fortress Press, 1995.

———. *Mystery and Hermeneutics. Part Two: Faith, Hermeneutics, and Word*. Edited by Milena Carrara Pavan. Maryknoll, NY: Orbis Books, 2021.

———. *Mysticism and Spirituality, Part One: Mysticism, the Fullness of Life*. Edited by Milena Carrara Pavan. Maryknoll, NY: Orbis Books, 2014.

———. *Mysticism and Spirituality, Part Two: Spirituality, the Way of Life*. Edited by Milena Carrara Pavan. Maryknoll, NY: Orbis Books, 2014.

———. "Raimon Panikkar: The Foundations of Democracy and the Discovery of the Metapolitical." *Interculture* 136 (April 1999): 30.

———. *Religion and Religions*. Maryknoll, NY: Orbis Books, 2015.

———. *The Rhythm of Being: The Unbroken Trinity*. Maryknoll, NY: Orbis Books, 2010.

———. *Sacred Secularity*. Edited by Milena Carrara Pavan. Maryknoll, NY: Orbis Books, 2022.

———. *Trinitarian and Cosmotheandric Vision*. Edited by Milena Carrara Pavan. Maryknoll, NY: Orbis Books, 2021.

———. *The Water of the Drop: Fragments from Panikkar's Diaries*. Edited by Milena Carrara Pavan. Delhi: Indian Society for Promoting Christian Knowledge, 2018.

———. *Worship and Secular Man: An Essay on the Liturgical Nature of Man, Considering Secularization as a Major Phenomenon of Our Time and Worship as an Apparent Fact of All Times: A Study towards an Integral Anthropology*. London: Darton, 1973.

Panikkar, Raimon, and Milena Carrara Pavan. *A Pilgrimage to Kailash*. New Delhi: Motilal Banarsidass, 2018.

Panikkar, Raimon, and Arvind Sharma. *Human Rights as a Western Concept*. New Delhi: D.K. Printworld, 2007.

Panko, Stephen M. *Martin Buber*. Makers of the Modern Theological Mind. Waco, TX: Word Books, 1976.

Paragg, Jillian. "'What Are You?': Mixed Race Responses to the Racial Gaze." *Ethnicities* 17, no. 3 (2015). https://journals.sagepub.com/doi/abs/10.1177/1468796815621938.

Park, Andrew Sung. *Racial Conflict and Healing: An Asian-American Theological Perspective*. Eugene, OR: Wipf & Stock, 2009.

Patton, Michael Quinn. *Qualitative Research & Evaluation Methods: Integrating Theory and Practice*. 4th ed. Thousand Oaks, CA: Sage Publications, 2015.

Pauker, Kristin, Chanel Meyers, Diana T. Sanchez, Sarah E. Gaither, and Danielle M. Young. "A Review of Multiracial Malleability: Identity, Categorization, and Shifting Racial Attitudes." *Social and Personality Psychology Compass* 12, no. 6 (June 2018): e12392. https://doi.org/10.1111/spc3.12392.

Pavan, Milena Carrara. Introduction to *Fullness of Life*. Edited by Kala Acharya, Milena Carrara Pavan, and William Parker, xv–xix. Mumbai: Somaiya Publications, 2008.

———. "Opera Omnia: The Philosophical and Spiritual Pilgrimage of Raimon Panikkar in Dialogue with Other Cultures and Religions." In *Raimundo Panikkar: A Pilgrim across Worlds*. Edited by Kapila Vatsyayan and Côme Carpentier de Gourdon, 135–46. New Delhi: Niyogi Books, 2016.

———. "Raimon Panikkar: Life and Work." In *Raimon Panikkar: A Companion to His Life and Thought*. Edited by Peter Phan and Young-chan Ro, 1–18. Cambridge, UK: James Clarke, 2020.

Pedrioli, Carlo A. "Under a Critical Race Theory Lens—Brown v. Board of Education: A Civil Rights Milestone and Its Troubled Legacy." *African American Law & Policy Report* 93 (2005): 15.

Phan, Peter C., and Young-chan Ro, eds. *Raimon Panikkar: A Companion to His Life and Thought*. Cambridge, UK: James Clarke, 2018.

Poling, James N., and Donald E. Miller. *Foundations for a Practical Theology of Ministry*. Nashville: Abingdon Press, 1985.

Pollard, Alton B. *Mysticism and Social Change: The Social Witness of Howard Thurman*. Martin Luther King, Jr. Memorial Studies in Religion, Culture, and Social Development 2. New York: P. Lang, 1992.

Poston, W. S. Carlos. "The Biracial Identity Development Model: A Needed Addition." *Journal of Counseling & Development* 69, no. 2 (November 12, 1990): 152–55. https://doi.org/10.1002/j.1556–6676.1990.tb01477.x.

Potter, Gina A. "The Invisibility of Multiracial Students: An Emerging Majority by 2050." EdD diss., UC San Diego, 2009. https://escholarship.org/uc/item/3p3240kx.

Powell, John. "Lessons from Suffering: How Social Justice Informs Spirituality." *University of St. Thomas Law Journal* 1, no. 1 (2003): 102.

Prabhu, Joseph. Foreword to *The Rhythm of Being: The Gifford Lectures*, xv–xvi. Maryknoll, NY: Orbis Books, 2010.

———. "Panikkar the Christian Thinker." In *Raimon Panikkar: A Companion to His Life and Thought*. Edited by Peter Phan and Young-chan Ro, 19–36. Cambridge, UK: James Clarke, 2020.

———. "Raimon Panikkar, Apostle of Inter-Faith Dialogue Dies." *National Catholic Reporter*, 2010. https://www.ncronline.org/news/spirituality/raimon-panikkar-apostle-interfaith-dialogue-dies.

———. "Roots, Routes, and a New Awakening: Walking and Meditating with Raimon Panikkar." In *Roots, Routes and a New Awakening: Beyond One and Many and Alternative Planetary Futures*. Edited by Ananta Kumar Giri, 193–200. Singapore: Palgrave Macmillan, 2021.

Pujol, Oscar. "The Intercultural Adventure of the Third Millennium: A Homage to Raimon Panikkar." In *Raimundo Panikkar: A Pilgrim across Worlds*. Edited by Kapila Vatsyayan and Côme Carpentier de Gourdon, 180–97. New Delhi: Niyogi Books, 2016.

Raimon Panikkar, 2018. https://vimeo.com/306270786.

Raimon Panikkar: The Window. https://www.youtube.com.

Renn, Kristen A. "Research on Biracial and Multiracial Identity Development: Overview and Synthesis." *New Directions for Student Services* 123 (June 2008): 13–21. https://doi.org/10.1002/ss.282.

Rockquemore, Kerry Ann, David L. Brunsma, and Daniel J. Delgado. "Racing to Theory or Retheorizing Race? Understanding the Struggle to Build a Multiracial Identity Theory." *Journal of Social Issues* 65, no. 1 (March 2009): 13–34. https://doi.org/10.1111/j.1540–4560.2008.01585.x.

Rogers, Frank, Jr. *Practicing Compassion*. Nashville, TN: Upper Room, 2015.

———. "TSF 4026 'Psycho-Spiritual Approaches to Contemplative Transformation' Class Notes," Claremont School of Theology, Spring 2017.

———. "TSF 4097 'The Way of Radical Compassion' Class Notes," Claremont School of Theology, Spring 2018.

———. "Warriors of Compassion: Coordinates on the Compass of Compassion-Based Activism." In Jennifer Baldwin, ed., *Taking It to the Streets: Public Theologies of Activism and Resistance* (Lanham, MD: Lexington Books, 2019), 25–42.

Rohr, Richard. *Everything Belongs: The Gift of Contemplative Prayer*. Rev. and updated ed. New York: Crossroad Publishing, 2003.

Sanchez, Diana T., Sarah E. Gaither, Analia F. Albuja, and Zoey Eddy. "How Policies Can Address Multiracial Stigma." *Policy Insights from the Behavioral and Brain Sciences* 7, no. 2 (October 2020): 115–22. https://doi.org/10.1177/2372732220943906.

Sanchez, Diana T., Margaret Shih, and Julie A. Garcia. "Juggling Multiple Racial Identities: Malleable Racial Identification and Psychological Well-Being." *Cultural Diversity and Ethnic Minority Psychology* 15, no. 3 (July 2009): 243–54. https://doi.org/10.1037/a0014373.

Sechrest, Love L., Johnny Ramírez-Johnson, and Amos Yong, eds. *Can "White" People Be Saved? Triangulating Race, Theology, and*

Mission. Missiological Engagements. Downers Grove, IL: IVP Academic, 2018.

Shih, Margaret, and Diana T. Sanchez. "When Race Becomes Even More Complex: Toward Understanding the Landscape of Multiracial Identity and Experiences." *Journal of Social Issues* 65, no. 1 (March 2009): 1–11. https://doi.org/10.1111/j.1540-4560.2008.01584.x.

Shrivastava, Aseem. "A Time for Ecosophy." *Open Magazine* (blog), May 1, 2020. https://openthemagazine.com/essays/a-time-for-ecosophy/.

Smith, Linda Tuhiwai. *Decolonizing Methodologies: Research and Indigenous Peoples*. 2nd ed. London: Zed Books, 2012.

Soars, Daniel, and Nadya Pohran, eds. *Hindu-Christian Dual Belonging*. Routledge Hindu Studies Series. New York: Routledge, 2022.

"Swami Abhishiktananda: An Interview with Raimon Panikkar—YouTube." https://www.youtube.com/watch?v=SOMcDuHh31g.

Swinton, John. *Raging with Compassion: Pastoral Responses to the Problem of Evil*. Grand Rapids, MI: William B. Eerdmans, 2007.

Swinton, John, and Harriet Mowat. *Practical Theology and Qualitative Research*. 2nd rev. ed. London: SCM, 2016.

Tetteh, Ishmael. "Nature as a Teacher." https://www.blogtalkradio.com/life-conversations/2012/05/10/ask-life-coach-ade-show.

Thurman, Howard. *Disciplines of the Spirit*. Richmond, IN: Friends United Press, 2003.

———. *Jesus and the Disinherited*. Boston: Beacon Press, 1996.

———. *Meditations of the Heart*. Boston: Beacon Press, 1999.

Thurman, Howard, and Luther E. Smith. *Howard Thurman: Essential Writings*. Modern Spiritual Masters. Maryknoll, NY: Orbis Books, 2006.

Thurston, Angie, and Casper ter Kuile. "CrossFit as Church? Examining How We Gather." https://news-archive.hds.harvard. edu/news/2015/11/04/crossfit-church-examining-how-we-gather.

Tillich, Paul. *Dynamics of Faith*. Perennial Classics. New York: Perennial, 2001.

Törngren, Sayaka Osanami, Nahikari Irastorza, and Dan Rodríguez-García. "Understanding Multiethnic and Multiracial Experiences Globally: Towards a Conceptual Framework of Mixedness." *Journal of Ethnic and Migration Studies* 47, no. 4 (March 12, 2021): 763–81. https://doi.org/10.1080/1369183X.2019.1654150.

Torres, Vasti, Susan R. Jones, and Kristen A. Renn. "Identity Development Theories in Student Affairs: Origins, Current Status, and New Approaches." *Journal of College Student Development* 50, no. 6 (2009): 577–96. https://doi.org/10.1353/csd.0.0102.

Townsend, Sarah S. M., Hazel R. Markus, and Hilary B. Bergsieker. "My Choice, Your Categories: The Denial of Multiracial Identities." *Journal of Social Issues* 65, no. 1 (March 2009): 185–204. https://doi.org/10.1111/j.1540–4560.2008. 01594.x.

Vatsyayan, Kapila, and Côme Carpentier de Gourdon, eds. *Raimundo Panikkar: A Pilgrim across Worlds*. New Delhi: Niyogi Books, 2016.

Vergés Gifra, Joan, ed. *Raimon Panikkar: Intercultural and Interreligious Dialogue*. Noms de La Filosofia Catalana 12. Girona: Documenta Universitaria, 2017.

Viswas, K. Maria Delasal. "Understanding Advaita: A Panikkarean Perspective for a Cross Cultural Journey." *Tattva Journal of Philosophy* 13, no. 1 (September 21, 2021): 77–91. https://doi.org/10.12726/tjp.25.6.

Vries, Kylan Mattias de, and Carey Jean Sojka. "Transitioning Gender, Transitioning Race: Transgender People and Multiracial Positionality." *International Journal of Transgender Health*, November 8, 2020, 1–11. https://doi.org/10.1080/26895269.2020.1838388.

Wallis, Jim. *America's Original Sin: Racism, White Privilege, and the Bridge to a New America*. Grand Rapids, MI: Baker Book House, 2017.

Wann, Chelsea Guillermo. *Examining Discrimination and Bias in the Campus Racial Climate: Multiple Approaches and Implications for the Use of Multiracial College Student Data*, 2012. https://eric.ed.gov/?id=ED538028.

———. "(Mixed) Race Matters: Racial Theory, Classification, and Campus Climate." UCLA, 2012. https://escholarship.org/uc/item/5jn7f86z.

———. *(Mixed) Race Matters: Racial Theory, Classification, and Campus Climate*. ProQuest. http://www.proquest.com/en-US/products/dissertations/individuals.shtml, 2013.

———. "Rethinking Research on Multiracial College Students," 2012, 53. https://eric.ed.gov.

Wijeyesinghe, Charmaine, and Bailey W. Jackson, eds. *New Perspectives on Racial Identity Development: Integrating Emerging Frameworks*. 2nd ed. New York: New York University Press, 2012.

Williams, angel Kyodo, Rod Owens, and Jasmine Syedullah. *Radical Dharma: Talking Race, Love, and Liberation*. Berkeley, CA: North Atlantic Books, 2016.

Williams, Patricia J. *The Alchemy of Race and Rights*. Cambridge, MA: Harvard University Press, 1991.

Williams, Rowan. Foreword to *Raimon Panikkar: A Companion to His Life and Thought*. Edited by Peter Phan and Young-chan Ro, xv–xviii. Cambridge, UK: James Clarke, 2020.

Wink, Walter. *Jesus and Nonviolence: A Third Way*. Minneapolis, MN: Fortress Press, 2003. http://public.eblib.com/choice/publicfullrecord.aspx?p=3380732.

Winters, Loretta I., and Herman L. DeBose, eds. *New Faces in a Changing America: Multiracial Identity in the 21st Century*. Thousand Oaks, CA: Sage Publications, 2003.

Yong, Aizaiah G. "All Mixed Up: Multi/Racial Liberation and Compassion-Based Activism." *Religions* 11, no. 8 (2020): 402. https://doi.org/10.3390/rel11080402.

———. "Critical Race Theory Meets Internal Family Systems: Toward a Compassion Spirituality for a Multireligious and

Multiracial World." *Buddhist-Christian Studies* 40, no. 1 (2020): 439–47. https://doi.org/10.1353/bcs.2020.0024.

———. "Decolonizing Pastoral Care in the Classroom: An Invitation to a Pedagogy of Spirit Experience." *Teaching Theology & Religion* 24, no. 2 (June 2021): 107–16. https://doi.org/10.1111/teth.12585.

Yong, Aizaiah G., and Nereyda S. Yong. "Parenting at Home: Reimagining Pastoral Theology during a Global Pandemic." *Feminist Studies in Religion* blog (January 12, 2022).

Yong, Amos, and Aizaiah G. Yong. "Seeking Healing in an Age of Partisan Division: Reckoning with Theological Education and Resounding the Evangel for the 2020s." In *Faith and Reckoning after Trump*. Edited by Miguel A. De La Torre, 214–27. Maryknoll, NY: Orbis Books, 2021.

Yusa, Michiko. "Intercultural Philosophical Wayfaring: An Autobiographical Account in Conversation with a Friend." *Journal of World Philosophies* 3, no. 1 (May 31, 2018): 123–34.

Index